JUMP START CSS

BY LOUIS LAZARIS

Jump Start CSS

by Louis Lazaris

Copyright © 2013 SitePoint Pty. Ltd.

Product Manager: Simon Mackie   **English Editor**: Paul Fitzpatrick

Technical Editor: Rachel Andrew   **Cover Designer**: Alex Walker

◆ sitepoint

Published by SitePoint Pty. Ltd.

48 Cambridge Street Collingwood
VIC Australia 3066
Web: www.sitepoint.com
Email: business@sitepoint.com

ISBN 978-0-9874674-4-7 (print)

ISBN 978-0-9874674-5-4 (ebook)
Printed and bound in the United States of America

About Louis Lazaris

Louis Lazaris is a web designer and blogger who has been creating and coding websites for more than a decade. You can find him on Twitter[1] or you can read more on CSS on his website, Impressive Webs[2].

About SitePoint

SitePoint specializes in publishing fun, practical, and easy-to-understand content for web professionals. Visit http://www.sitepoint.com/ to access our blogs, books, newsletters, articles, and community forums. You'll find a stack of information on JavaScript, PHP, Ruby, mobile development, design, and more.

About Jump Start

Jump Start books provide you with a rapid and practical introduction to web development languages and technologies. Typically around 150 pages in length, they can be read in a weekend, giving you a solid grounding in the topic and the confidence to experiment on your own.

---

[1] https://twitter.com/ ImpressiveWebs
[2] http://www.impressivewebs.com/

Table of Contents

Preface

Do you remember your first educational toy? One of the first that many children get is the big, chunky puzzle—four to ten easy-to-grip pieces that fit into spaces on a board.

This is one of the first experiences a child has with matching shapes to corresponding spaces, helping them develop their shape recognition skills.

My wife thinks I was never given one of these puzzles. Every time I put the dishes away, the plastic food storage containers stump me. I end up trying to put medium containers into small containers and square containers into round ones. It's as if, in her words, I never got the proper training as a child. I pretend she's just joking, but maybe she's right—I really can't remember.

If you've purchased this little book, in terms of CSS knowledge, you're a lot like an infant with its first shapes puzzle. I hope to teach you as much as possible, as quickly as possible, about the fundamentals of CSS. And I hope later in life you'll look back and be thankful that you took the time to "learn your shapes."

Who Should Read This Book

This book is suitable for beginner level web designers and developers. Some knowledge of HTML is assumed.

Conventions Used

You'll notice that we've used certain typographic and layout styles throughout this book to signify different types of information. Look out for the following items.

Code Samples

Code in this book will be displayed using a fixed-width font, like so:

```
<h1>A Perfect Summer's Day</h1>
<p>It was a lovely day for a walk in the park. The birds
were singing and the kids were all back at school.</p>
```

If the code is to be found in the book's code archive, the name of the file will appear at the top of the program listing, like this:

```
                                                                    example.css
.footer {
  background-color: #CCC;
  border-top: 1px solid #333;
}
```

If only part of the file is displayed, this is indicated by the word *excerpt*:

```
                                                            example.css (excerpt)
  border-top: 1px solid #333;
```

If additional code is to be inserted into an existing example, the new code will be displayed in bold:

```
function animate() {
  new_variable = "Hello";
}
```

Also, where existing code is required for context, rather than repeat all it, a ⋮ will be displayed:

```
function animate() {
  ⋮
  return new_variable;
}
```

Some lines of code are intended to be entered on one line, but we've had to wrap them because of page constraints. A ➥ indicates a line break that exists for formatting purposes only, and that should be ignored.

```
URL.open("http://www.sitepoint.com/responsive-web-design-real-user-
➥testing/?responsive1");
```

Tips, Notes, and Warnings

Hey, You!

Tips will give you helpful little pointers.

Ahem, Excuse Me ...

Notes are useful asides that are related—but not critical—to the topic at hand. Think of them as extra tidbits of information.

Make Sure You Always ...

... pay attention to these important points.

Watch Out!

Warnings will highlight any gotchas that are likely to trip you up along the way.

Supplementary Materials

http://www.sitepoint.com/books/jscss1/
The book's website, containing links, updates, resources, and more.

http://www.sitepoint.com/books/jscss1/code.php
The downloadable code archive for this book.

http://www.sitepoint.com/forums/forumdisplay.php?53-css
SitePoint's forums, for help on any tricky web problems.

books@sitepoint.com
Our email address, should you need to contact us for support, to report a problem, or for any other reason.

Want to take your learning further?

Thanks for buying this book. We appreciate your support. Do you want to continue learning? You can now get unlimited access to courses and ALL SitePoint books at

Learnable for one low price. Enroll now and start learning today! Join Learnable and you'll stay ahead of the newest technology trends: http://www.learnable.com.

Acknowledgments

Thanks to Simon Mackie and Rachel Andrew for their excellent and practical feedback to help make this book much better than it would have been had I tackled this on my own.

Chapter 1

An Introduction to CSS

Welcome to Jump Start CSS! This book is an introduction to CSS that'll teach you the basics so you can start sprucing up your web pages using Cascading Style Sheets (CSS), the industry standard technology for formatting web pages.

For the most part, this book will not serve as a theoretical source for the topics we'll be discussing—there are plenty of other resources for that. In this brief volume, we'll be focusing on practical information. I'll be showing you, in rapid fashion, what the various aspects of CSS are, and how you can use them to build web pages.

The Sample Project

In order to give you hands-on experience with CSS, this book is centered around a sample project that we'll be building together.

The sample project is a phony website called RecipeFinder. You can access a completed version of that website by visiting http://spbooks.github.io/JSCSS1/ in any web browser.

We're going to take RecipeFinder from mock-up to development. The sample site's look is based on a Photoshop design. Figure 1.1 shows you what it looks like.

Figure 1.1. The website we'll be building in this book

Now, before we get into building our project, let's properly introduce the elements of CSS and how it's used to style web pages.

How are web pages built?

Let's begin by briefly considering what exactly CSS is, and how it relates to a web page. Web pages are built on **content**. Content is what you see when you visit a page. It might include text, photos, graphics, and video. Content is stored using a language called HTML. You've probably heard of it, but here's a very quick overview.

HTML consists of **elements**, many of which have what are called opening and closing **tags**. These instruct web browsers how content (copy, photos, videos, and so on) should be presented on screen. For example:

```
<header>
<h1>RecipeFinder</h1>
</header>
```

In this case, the content that's visible on the page is the text "RecipeFinder." Everything else you see there (specifically the information inside the angle brackets) is HTML, and it's invisible on the page when viewed in a browser. What it does is to help mark where sections of content begin and end. For this reason **HTML** is what's called a markup language. In fact, it stands for Hyper Text Markup Language.

As mentioned, this is not a book on HTML, but if you want to learn more, two possible resources are SitePoint's online HTML Concepts[1] or the Mozilla Developer Network's Introduction to HTML.[2]

What Is CSS?

CSS stands for Cascading Style Sheets and is a separate, but complementary, language to HTML. CSS is what we use to apply styles to the content on our web page.

Let's use the HTML from the example above to give you a first taste of CSS. Don't worry if this looks foreign to you right now—just become familiar with the look of the code:

```
header {
    color: white;
    background-color: #333;
    font-size: 1.5em;
}
```

What you see above is referred to as a **rule set**. Notice the curly braces that wrap three lines of code. Also, notice that each line inside the curly braces has a colon and a semi-colon. Everything inside the curly braces is called a **declaration block**.

---

[1] http://reference.sitepoint.com/html/html-concepts
[2] https://developer.mozilla.org/en-US/docs/HTML/Introduction

The portion prior to the first curly brace is what defines which part of the web page we are styling. This is referred to as the **selector**. We'll discuss more on selectors later in this chapter. In this case, our CSS is targeting the `<header>` HTML element.

Each of the three lines in the declaration block is referred to as a—you guessed it—**declaration**. Additionally, each declaration consists of a **property** (the part before the colon) and a **value** (the part after the colon). Finally, each CSS declaration ends with a semi-colon.

What I've shown you here is a very simple example. Other CSS code examples might be more complex, but most are fairly easy to figure out through trial and error—so don't be too intimidated if you come across something you don't recognize.

So what does that code do? Well, we'll get into the specifics on CSS properties later, so hang tight while we continue discussing some further important basics that'll serve as a foundation for the rest of this book.

How do I include CSS in a web page?

CSS can be inserted into a web page in four different ways. Let's take a look at each one, saving the most highly recommended method for last.

Using Inline Styles

Any HTML element on a web page can be styled using **inline styles**. Here's an example, using some of the HTML we've already introduced:

```
<h1 style="color: blue; background-color:
#333;">RecipeFinder</h1>
```

In this case, the CSS is contained inside of an HTML **attribute** called `style`. The attribute tells the browser that what follows inside the quotation marks is CSS. In this example, the styles will only apply to the element to which they're attached (the `<h1>` element in this case). This is a very inefficient way of inserting CSS and should be avoided in almost all circumstances.

Using the `<style>` Element

You can also include CSS in an HTML page using a `<style>` tag, which also requires a closing `</style>` tag:

```
<style>
header {
    color: white;
    background-color: #333;
    font-size: 1.5em;
}
</style>
```

In this example, the styles will apply only to the element(s) targeted in the selector. So, in this instance, the styles will apply to all <header> elements on the page where this <style> element appears.

Using @import inside a <style> element

You also have the option to include CSS in a separate file. It's similar to a text file, but has a file extension of ".css". So a chunk of CSS inside a separate file can be imported into your HTML like this:

```
<style>
@import url(css/style.css);
</style>
```

The @import method of including CSS has been known to cause some problems—for example, multiple CSS files loaded via @import will often take longer to download[3]—so, in general, you'd do well to avoid using it.

The Best Way: Using the <link> Element

The best way to include CSS in a web page is by means of the <link> element:

```
<link rel="stylesheet" href="css/style.css">
```

This element, which would be placed in the <head> element of your HTML document, is much like @import in that it references an external file. This enables you to keep all your CSS code separate from the HTML. In addition, this method doesn't cause some of the issues that can arise when using @import. Also, because the styles are not "inline," scattered among the HTML, your CSS will be that much easier to maintain.

---

[3] http://www.stevesouders.com/blog/2009/04/09/dont-use-import/

Introducing CSS Selectors

As already alluded to, a CSS selector is the part of a CSS rule set that actually selects the content you want to style. Let's look at all the different kinds of selectors available, with a brief description of each.

Universal Selector

The **universal selector** works like a wild card character, selecting all elements on a page. You'll recall, from our brief overview earlier, that every HTML page is built on content placed within HTML tags. Each set of tags represents an element on the page. Look at the following CSS example, which uses the universal selector:

```
* {
    color: green;
    font-size: 20px;
    line-height: 25px;
}
```

The three lines of code inside the curly braces (`color`, `font-size`, and `line-height`) will apply to all elements on the HTML page. As seen here, the universal selector is declared using an asterisk. You can also use the universal selector in combination with other selectors—something we'll discuss a little later in this chapter.

Element Type Selector

Also referred to simply as a "type selector," this selector must match one or more HTML elements of the same name. Thus, a selector of `nav` would match all HTML `<nav>` elements, and a selector of `ul` would match all HTML unordered lists, or `<ul>` elements.

The following example uses an element type selector to match all `<ul>` elements:

```
ul {
    list-style: none;
    border: solid 1px #ccc;
}
```

To put this in some context, here's a section of HTML to which we'll apply the above CSS:

```
<ul>
  <li>Fish</li>
  <li>Apples</li>
  <li>Cheese</li>
</ul>

<div class="example">
  <p>Example paragraph text.</p>
</div>

<ul>
  <li>Water</li>
  <li>Juice</li>
  <li>Maple Syrup</li>
</ul>
```

There are three main elements making up this part of the page: Two `<ul>` elements and a `<div>`. The CSS will apply only to the two `<ul>` elements, and not to the `<div>`. Were we to change the element type selector to use div instead of ul, then the styles would apply to the `<div>` and not to the two `<ul>` elements.

Also note that the styles will not apply to the elements *inside* the `<ul>` or `<div>` elements. That being said, some of the styles *may* be inherited by those inner elements—more on this later in the book.

ID Selector

An ID selector is declared using a hash, or pound symbol (#) preceding a string of characters. The string of characters is defined by the developer. This selector matches any HTML element that has an ID attribute with the same value as that of the selector, but minus the hash symbol.

Here's an example:

```
#container {
    width: 960px;
    margin: 0 auto;
}
```

This CSS uses an ID selector to match an HTML element such as:

```
<div id="container"></div>
```

In this case, the fact that this is a `<div>` element doesn't matter—it could be any kind of HTML element. As long as it has an ID attribute with a value of `container`, the styles will apply.

An ID element on a web page should be unique. That is, there should only be a single element on any given page with an ID of `container`. This makes the ID selector quite inflexible, because the styles used in the ID selector rule set can be used only once per page.

If there happens to be more than one element on the page with the same ID, the styles will still apply, but the HTML on such a page would be invalid from a technical standpoint, so you'll want to avoid doing this.

In addition to the problems of inflexibility, ID selectors also have the problem of very high specificity—an issue we'll be talking about later in this chapter.

Class Selector

The class selector is the most useful of all CSS selectors. It's declared with a dot preceding a string of one or more characters. Just as is the case with an ID selector, this string of characters is defined by the developer. The class selector also matches all elements on the page that have their class attribute set to the same value as the class, minus the dot.

Take the following rule set:

```
.box {
    padding: 20px;
    margin: 10px;
    width: 240px;
}
```

These styles will apply to the following HTML element:

```
<div class="box"></div>
```

The same styles will also apply to any other HTML elements that have a class attribute with a value of box. Having multiple elements on a single page with the same class attribute is beneficial, because it allows you to reuse styles, and avoid needless repetition. In addition to this, class selectors have very low specificity—again, more on this later.

Another reason the class selector is a valuable ally is that HTML allows multiple classes to be added to a single element. This is done by separating the classes in the HTML class attribute using spaces. Here's an example:

```
<div class="box box-more box-extended"></div>
```

Descendant Combinator

The descendant selector or, more accurately, the descendant **combinator** lets you combine two or more selectors so you can be more specific in your selection method. For example:

```
#container .box {
    float: left;
    padding-bottom: 15px;
}
```

This declaration block will apply to all elements that have a class of box that are inside an element with an ID of container. It's worth noting that the .box element doesn't have to be an immediate child: there could be another element wrapping .box, and the styles would still apply.

Look at the following HTML:

```
<div id="container">
  <div class="box"></div>

  <div class="box-2"></div>
</div>

<div class="box"></div>
```

If we apply the CSS in the previous example to this section of HTML, the only element that'll be affected by those styles is the first <div> element that has a class of box. The <div> element that has a class of box-2 *won't* be affected by the styles.

Similarly, the second `<div>` element with a class of `box` won't be affected because it's not inside an element with an ID of `container`.

You should be careful when using the descendant combinator in your CSS. This kind of selector, while making your CSS a little easier to read, can unnecessarily restrict your styles to a specific context—in this case, the styles are restricted to boxes inside of `#container`—which can make your code inflexible.

Child Combinator

A selector that uses the child combinator is similar to a selector that uses a descendant combinator, except it only targets immediate child elements:

```
#container > .box {
    float: left;
    padding-bottom: 15px;
}
```

This is the same code from the descendant combinator example, but instead of a space character, we're using the greater-than symbol (or right angle bracket.)

In this example, the selector will match all elements that have a class of `box` and that are *immediate children* of the `#container` element. That means, unlike the descendant combinator, there can't be another element wrapping `.box`—it has to be a direct child element.

Here's an HTML example:

```
<div id="container">
  <div class="box"></div>

  <div>
     <div class="box"></div>
  </div>
</div>
```

In this example, the CSS from the previous code example will apply only to the first `<div>` element that has a class of `box`. As you can see, the second `<div>` element with a class of `box` is inside another `<div>` element. As a result, the styles will not apply to that element, even though it too has a class of `box`.

Again, selectors that use this combinator can be somewhat restricting, but they can come in handy—for example, when styling nested lists.

General Sibling Combinator

A selector that uses a general sibling combinator matches elements based on sibling relationships. That is to say, the selected elements are beside each other in the HTML.

```
h2 ~ p {
    margin-bottom: 20px;
}
```

This type of selector is declared using the tilde character (~). In this example, all paragraph elements (<p>) will be styled with the specified rules, but only if they are siblings of <h2> elements. There could be other elements in between the <h2> and <p>, and the styles would still apply.

Let's apply the CSS from above to the following HTML:

```
<h2>Title</h2>
<p>Paragraph example.</p>
<p>Paragraph example.</p>
<p>Paragraph example.</p>
<div class="box">
  <p>Paragraph example.</p>
</div>
```

In this example, the styles will apply only to the first three paragraph elements. The last paragraph element is not a sibling of the <h2> element because it sits inside the <div> element.

Adjacent Sibling Combinator

A selector that uses the adjacent sibling combinator uses the plus symbol (+), and is almost the same as the general sibling selector. The difference is that the targeted element must be an *immediate* sibling, not just a general sibling. Let's see what the CSS code for this looks like:

```
p + p {
    text-indent: 1.5em;
    margin-bottom: 0;
}
```

This example will apply the specified styles only to paragraph elements that imme-diately follow other paragraph elements. This means the first paragraph element on a page would not receive these styles. Also, if another element appeared between two paragraphs, the second paragraph of the two wouldn't have the styles applied.

So, if we apply this selector to the following HTML:

```
<h2>Title</h2>
<p>Paragraph example.</p>
<p>Paragraph example.</p>
<p>Paragraph example.</p>

<div class="box">
  <p>Paragraph example.</p>
  <p>Paragraph example.</p>
</div>
```

...the styles will apply only to the second, third, and fifth paragraphs in this section of HTML.

Attribute Selector

The attribute selector targets elements based on the presence and/or value of HTML attributes, and is declared using square brackets:

```
input[type="text"] {
    background-color: #444;
    width: 200px;
}
```

There should not be a space before the opening square bracket unless you intend to use it along with a descendant combinator. The above CSS would match the fol-lowing element:

```
<input type="text">
```

But it wouldn't match this one:

```
<input type="submit">
```

The attribute selector can also be declared using just the attribute itself, with no value, like this:

```
input[type] {
    background-color: #444;
    width: 200px;
}
```

This will match all input elements with an attribute of `type`, regardless of the value.

You can also use attribute selectors without specifying anything outside the square brackets (thus targeting based on the attribute alone, irrespective of the element). It's also worth noting that, when using values, you have the option to include quotes (single or double,) or not.

Pseudo-class

A pseudo-class uses a colon character to identify a pseudo-state that an element might be in—for example, the state of being hovered, or the state of being activated. Let's look at a common example:

```
a:hover {
    color: red;
}
```

In this case, the pseudo-class portion of the selector is the `:hover` part. Here we've attached this pseudo-class to all anchor elements (`<a>` elements). This means that when the user hovers their mouse over an `<a>` element, the color property for that element will change to red. This type of pseudo-class is a dynamic pseudo-class, because it occurs only in response to user interaction—in this case, the mouse moving over the targeted element.

It's important to recognize that these types of selectors do not just select elements; they select elements that are in a particular state. For the purposes of this example, the state is the "hover" state. We'll look at other examples of pseudo-classes later in the book.

Pseudo-element

Finally, CSS has a selector referred to as a pseudo-element and, used appropriately, it can be very useful. The only caveat is that this selector is quite different from the other examples we've considered. Let's see a pseudo-element in context:

```css
.container:before {
    content: "";
    display: block;
    width: 50px;
    height: 50px;
    background-color: #141414;
}
```

This example uses one kind of pseudo-element, the `:before` pseudo-element. As the name suggests, this selector inserts an imaginary element into the page, inside the targeted element, before its contents.

Don't worry—we'll cover pseudo-elements in greater detail later in the book.

Using Multiple Selectors

Each of the selectors shown above can be combined with one or more other selectors. For the most part, you'll want to avoid combining too many selectors together, but here are a few quick examples to help you grasp the concept:

```css
p.box {
    color: blue;
}
```

In this example, we're combining the element type selector with a class selector. As a result, this will target only paragraph elements that have a class of `.box`. This is a poor choice of selector, and should be avoided in almost all circumstances. In normal practice, it's more than enough to specify a selector with a class such as `.box` without over-qualifying it with the p portion (or any other element type selector).

```
#form [type=text] {
  border: solid 1px #ccc;
}
```

This selector combines the ID selector with the attribute selector. This will target all elements with a type attribute of text that are inside an element with an ID of form.

```
p, div, .box {
  color: black;
}
```

Here we're using commas to separate our selectors. This is a useful method to use to combine multiple selectors in a single rule set. In this case, the styles will apply to all paragraph elements, all <div> elements, and all elements that have a class of box.

The Cascade and Specificity

At first glance, the following concepts can seem difficult to grasp. But the truth is, if you're a CSS beginner, there are methods you can employ to ensure that they don't cause too many problems for you.

First, let's look at what we mean when we refer to style sheets as **cascading** and how **specificity** ties in.

Usually, when a browser interprets a CSS document, it does so from top to bottom, giving precedence—or overriding abilities—to the declarations that appear lower down in the document.

Let's look at a simple example so you can understand what I mean when discussing precedence and overriding abilities. Assume the following two declaration blocks appear in a single CSS file:

```
p {
  font-size: 20px;
}
```

```
p {
    font-size: 30px;
}
```

Here we're using the exact same selector for both rule sets—the element type selector, which targets all paragraph elements. The difference between these two rule sets, however, is the value of the font-size property. Here we're defining the font-size twice for the same element. So what will the size of the font actually be? Well, since the rule set that defines the font size at 30px appears after the previous rule set, then the font will be sized at 30px.

This is a very simple example, but it neatly demonstrates how selectors targeting styles later in a CSS document have precedence over the same selectors that appear earlier in the CSS file. Simple, right? Unfortunately, different selectors have different levels of specificity. Look at the following example:

```
div p {
    color: blue;
}

p {
    color: red;
}
```

If all the <p> elements on a web page were nested inside a <div>, the first rule set (which uses div p,) would always apply, overriding any of the same styles defined in the second rule set (which uses only p). This is because the descendant selector (used in the first example) takes precedence over the element type selector (used in the second example).

In this instance, the color value for paragraph elements inside of <div> elements will be blue—despite the fact that the second color declaration appears later in the document. So although the browser does give some importance to the order of these rule sets, that order is superseded by the specificity of the first rule set.

Here's another example:

```
#main {
    color: green;
}

body div.container {
    color: pink;
}
```

which assumes the following HTML:

```
<div id="main" class="container"></div>
```

In this case, it might seem that the second rule set, which uses two type selectors, a class selector and a descendant selector all in one, would have precedence over the first rule set, which only uses the ID selector. But this isn't the case. The color value on the container element would become green because the ID selector (used in the first example) has very high specificity and thus takes precedence over the second rule set.

It should be noted here that when we refer to the overriding of selectors and selectors taking precedence, we're assuming that the same styles are defined on these different rule sets. So, for example, in the previous code block, if the #main rule set defined color and the body `div.container` selector defined a different property, then they would both apply, because there'd be nothing being overridden. To recap, then: specificity does not affect all styles, but only the styles that are duplicated across multiple selectors.

This use of the ID selector—and its strong override abilities—clearly illustrates why it's important to avoid using it, wherever possible. Traditionally, CSS developers have encouraged the ID selector's use for unique elements, and, according to standards, it's a perfectly valid CSS selector. But please keep in mind that overusing it may cause all sorts of problems in the long run.

In order to avoid being tripped up by specificity, use the class selector widely and learn what's referred to as "Object Oriented CSS" or "modular CSS".[4]

---

[4] For more advanced learning on this subject, see SMACSS [http://smacss.com/] and An Introduction to Object Oriented CSS.
[http://coding.smashingmagazine.com/2011/12/12/an-introduction-to-object-oriented-css-oocss/]

Selective Treatment

The suggestion to avoid ID selectors only applies to IDs in CSS, not in HTML. ID attributes are absolutely necessary for local, or same-page, links and can be very useful when attempting to target elements using JavaScript.

Other selectors will also add certain levels of specificity, but not so much that they'll cause problems. If, for example, you have to target something with a pseudo-class or child selector, that's fine. Use those selectors whenever you find them to be practical.

There are a number of detailed articles online explaining cascade and specificity. These include a series on SitePoint's CSS Reference,[5] which are highly recommend once you've a good grasp of some of the basics introduced in this book.

Always Use Standards Mode

A basic rule of thumb is that every HTML document you create should use "standards mode." For a beginner, this might sound a bit too techy, but it's actually quite simple to ensure that all your HTML pages comply.

To ensure your CSS is rendered properly by the browser (meaning, it's in standards mode,) make sure the HTML document to which your styles are applying has the following tag at the top, before all other content:

```
<!doctype html>
```

That's it. This tag is referred to as an HTML5 document type declaration or "doctype." In older documents, you'll occasionally come across other lengthier doctypes, which are commonly used for XHTML or HTML4 web pages. For example:

```
<!DOCTYPE html PUBLIC "-//W3C//DTD XHTML 1.0
Strict//EN"
"http://www.w3.org/TR/xhtml1/DTD/xhtml1-strict.dtd">
```

---

[5] http://reference.sitepoint.com/css/inheritancecascade

You can do some further reading on doctypes at SitePoint's HTML reference[6] but, for now, all you need to know is that, if you use the simple HTML5 doctype, your pages will render in standards mode and your CSS will be much easier to code and debug.

A Skeleton for Our Sample Website

We've covered quite a bit of ground, already, without touching our sample project. Let's conclude this chapter by using some of the selectors we've learned about to build a CSS skeleton for the RecipeFinder website.

First, we need to add an external CSS file to our project that'll help us achieve similar results in almost all browsers and on any device. Of course, not every web browser supports every CSS feature (more on this later,) but we can make a fairly normalized cross-browser start to our project by using something called a "CSS reset."

What do we mean by "normalized cross-browser"? Well, every browser applies certain styles to elements on a web page by default. For example, if you use an unordered list (the `<ul>` element) the browser will display the list with some existing formatting styles, including bullets next to the individual list items (the `<li>` elements inside the `<ul>`). By using a CSS reset document at the top of your CSS file, you can reset all these styles to a bare minimum. To put it another way, it clears the ground before we start building something new.

At this stage, it's not necessary to understand everything in a CSS reset. Most experts wouldn't be able to speak intelligently on every line of CSS in such a document. The important thing to understand is that it's a valuable tool in your CSS arsenal, and it's imperative that you use one on every project to avoid as many cross-browser problems as possible.

That said, you can't just throw a CSS reset document into a pre-existing site, and expect it to "fix" everything. That's not how CSS resets work. A reset is designed to be used as a starting point, not as a quick-fix for existing websites that aren't behaving in different browsers.

---

[6] http://reference.sitepoint.com/html/doctypes

Two of the most popular CSS resets are Eric Meyer's Reset[7] and Nicolas Gallagher's Normalize.css.[8] Normalize.css is what we'll use as a foundation for our project. So our base HTML will look like this:

```
<!doctype html>
<html lang="en">
<head>
    <meta charset="utf-8">
    <title>RecipeFinder</title>

    <link rel="stylesheet" href="css/normalize.css">
    <link rel="stylesheet" href="css/styles.css">

    <!--[if lt IE 9]>
    <script src="http://html5shiv.googlecode.com/
➥svn/trunk/html5.js"></script>
    <![endif]-->
</head>
<body>
</body>
</html>
```

Notice the two CSS file references. One is **Normalize.css** and the other is the stylesheet that we're going to build. Remember what we talked about earlier regarding the cascade? To ensure that the Normalize.css styles work correctly, this file has to be referenced first, prior to any other CSS we add. This ensures that any styles we add later in the CSS will override whatever is in our **Normalize.css** file.

 The HTML5 Shiv

You'll probably notice in our HTML that we've included a `<script>` tag that references a file called **HTML5shiv**. This is necessary to enable older versions of Internet Explorer to apply CSS to all HTML5 tags. For more information on this, see this article by Remy Sharp.[9]

Now that we have that basic foundation in place, let's look at our RecipeFinder graphic again and decide how we want to divide up our page. Then we'll choose

---

[7] http://meyerweb.com/eric/tools/css/reset/

[8] http://necolas.github.com/normalize.css/

[9] http://remysharp.com/2009/01/07/html5-enabling-script/

some CSS selectors to attach to declaration blocks that we'll populate throughout the book.

Notice in Figure 1.2 the different sections of the website have been overlaid with colors, so you can envision roughly how the HTML structure will be defined.

Figure 1.2. The RecipeFinder website with colors indicating how we'll divide up the layout

We'll introduce the different parts of the HTML as we go along. For now, here's a bare skeleton CSS framework that we'll use:

```
a:link, a:visited {
}

a:hover {
}

h1 {
}

h2 {
}

body > header {
}

  nav ul {
  }

.promo {
}

.main {
}

  .latest {
  }
    .media {
    }
      .media img {
      }

  .sidebar {
  }

footer {
}
```

Right now, these are just bare declaration blocks with only selectors present, and no actual CSS styles. This framework won't affect the document yet, but simply serves to illustrate how we're going to use some of the selectors I've introduced in this chapter.

Here you can see we're making generous use of the class selector (e.g. .promo) and we've also included use of the element type selector (e.g. h1 and h2) as well as the descendant selector (e.g. .media img) and the child combinator (e.g. body > header).

You'll also notice another convention we've used here: portions of the CSS have been indented to match the indenting that will exist in the HTML itself. You don't have to do this, but it's a nice way to keep the CSS easy to scan when it starts building up.

If there's anything you don't understand in our CSS skeleton, don't worry too much about it right now. We'll go into more detail in the coming chapters as we put some meat on those bones, so to speak.

What about the HTML?

This book is not about HTML, so although there will be some code snippets showing what HTML we're dealing with when writing the CSS, the HTML will, for the most part, not be shown or discussed.

If you want to get the most out of the tutorial that runs through this book, I suggest that you download the code archive and use the HTML file provided in the download. You can remove the completed CSS file that's included with the archive and build your own CSS file step-by-step as you progress through the book.

All the code examples in this book, if patched together correctly, will build the complete CSS file (minus all the extra vendor prefixes for newer CSS features—more on this in Chapter 5).

Summary

In this chapter, you've learned about the different components of a CSS rule set, you've been introduced to the different ways to select elements via CSS, and you've had a glimpse of some relevant concepts with regards to the cascade and specificity.

I've also introduced the sample project, and we've put together a base CSS file that is preceded by a set of styles that normalizes some browser differences.

In the next chapter, we'll start putting together the structural foundation for the RecipeFinder website and, in the process, you'll learn about CSS-based layouts.

Layout Techniques

In this chapter, I'm going to introduce you to some layout techniques. You'll get hands-on experience with these when we implement some of them into the skeleton we built for our CSS in Chapter 1.

Before that, there are some additional fundamental concepts that we didn't cover in Chapter 1 that you'll get to know.

The Box Model

The box model refers to the (usually) invisible rectangular area that is created for each HTML element. This area has four basic components, and it's much easier to explain using a diagram, so take a look at Figure 2.1:

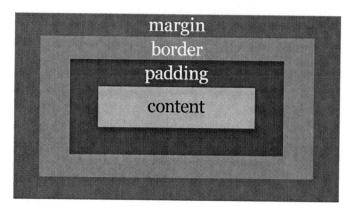

Figure 2.1. A graphic representation of the box model

The box model components in this diagram are exaggerated. Normally, the only large and visible area of any HTML element is the content area. Using this larger-than-life example, however, we can discuss each component, starting from the inside and working our way out:

Content   The content portion of the box model holds—you guessed it—the actual content. We introduced this briefly in Chapter 1 when discussing HTML elements. The content can be text, images, or whatever else is visible on a web page.

Padding   The padding of an element is defined using the padding property. The padding is the space around the content. It can be defined for an individual side (for example, `padding-left: 20px`) or for all four sides in one declaration—`padding: 20px 10px 30px 20px`, for instance. When declaring all four sides, you're using a **shorthand** property. There'll be more on shorthand later in the chapter. Often when a CSS property takes multiple values like this, they start at the top and go clockwise in relation to the element. So, in the example just cited, this would apply 20px of padding to the top, 10px to the right, 30px to the bottom, and 20px to the left.

Border   The border of an element is defined using the border property. This is a shorthand property that defines the element's `border-width`, `border-style`, and `border-color`. For example, `border: 4px dashed orange`.

Margin   Finally, the last part of the box model is the element's margin. Margins are similar to padding, and are defined using similar syntax (for example, `margin-left: 15px` or `margin: 10px 20px 10px 20px`). However, unlike padding, the margin portion of an element exists outside the element. A margin creates space between the targeted element and surrounding elements.

Every element on a web page has these box model components. Sometimes the default characteristics of these components differ on certain types of elements. For example, form elements start out with a certain width and height, even if you don't define those properties. Also, as mentioned in Chapter 1, unordered lists (`<ul>` elements,) will start out with predefined margins and padding due to the browser's internal stylesheet, even if those are not set in the CSS.

Block versus Inline

Another concept you should be familiar with is that most HTML elements fall under two categories: block or inline. A block-level element is more of a structural, layout-related element, while an inline-level element is usually found inside of block-level elements, flowing in the same context as text.

Block-level elements include elements like `<div>`, `<p>`, and `<section>`, whereas inline elements include `<span>`, `<b>`, and `<em>`. These are just a few examples.

Using CSS, you can change an element's default behavior in this regard by using the display property, like this:

```
span {
    display: block;
}
```

The behavior of block-level compared to that of inline-level elements isn't too tricky to grasp, and that understanding can be a rewarding "aha!" moment for many beginner CSS developers, so it's good to learn this concept early. Figure 2.2 visually demonstrates the difference between block and inline.

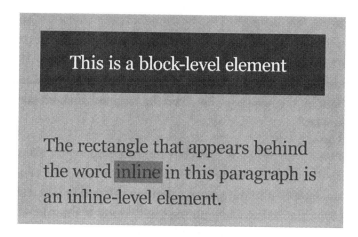

Figure 2.2. A visual demonstration of the difference between block and inline

Block elements have certain characteristics. First, unless given a specific width, they always expand horizontally to fit inside their parent container and will also, by default, expand vertically to hold their contents. So there is normally no need to, say, add a specific width to a block element unless you require its width to be smaller than the available space within its parent element. And there's rarely a need to give an explicit height to a block element since, in most cases, it will naturally expand to hold its contents.

As mentioned, block elements are structural-type elements and so will, by default, start below the elements on the page that appear before them in the HTML. This is an important part of understanding how they differ from inline elements.

In essence, inline elements behave like words and letters within of a paragraph. As you can see in Figure 2.2, an inline element will flow naturally with text, and usually it'll contain nothing but text or other inline elements. It's worth noting that inline elements are subject to CSS properties that affect text. For example, line-height and letter-spacing are CSS properties that can be used to style inline elements. However, those same properties wouldn't affect block elements.

Additionally, inline elements can't have specified width and height values, and they'll ignore top and bottom margins. That said, they can accept left and right margin values as well as any padding.

For reasons concerned with layout, you'll occasionally want to have something that somewhat resembles both block and inline. This is possible by setting an element to a value of `inline-block`, which you can do as follows:

```
.example {
    display: inline-block;
}
```

This gives us the best of both worlds—allowing the element to stay inline with text, and still be subject to text-based CSS, while at the same time accepting width, height, and margin values like a block element. Later in this chapter, we'll use inline-block to style the main navigation of our example site.

Shorthand versus Longhand CSS

Yet another important concept to understand is the difference between shorthand and longhand CSS properties. As we've already discussed, a single CSS declaration usually consists of a property followed by a colon, followed by a value, then a semicolon.

Shorthand properties work a bit differently. A shorthand property's value is actually a set of values, each of which maps to an existing CSS longhand property. Let's look at an example that we've already introduced—the `border` property:

```
.example {
    border: dashed 2px blue;
}
```

The rule set above, which contains just one declaration, can also be written in longhand, like this:

```
.example {
    border-style: dashed;
    border-width: 2px;
    border-color: blue;
}
```

From this it's easy to see why you'll rarely come across the longhand version of border-related properties. It's simpler to use the shorthand, and it uses less code, which, in a large CSS file, will make a small impact on page speed and probably a big impact on future code maintenance.

It should also be noted that if you leave out one of the values of a shorthand property, it will cause that value to revert to its initial, or default, state. Let's combine our previous two code examples so you can see how this works:

```
.example {
  border-style: dashed;
  border-width: 2px;
  border-color: blue;
}

.example {
  border: solid;
  color: green;
}
```

Here we've used the same selector on two different rule sets. As we learned in Chapter 1, the second rule set will take precedence over the first, overriding any styles that are the same in both rule sets.

In the first rule set, we've defined all three border-related properties in longhand, setting the values to display a dashed border that's 2px wide and colored blue. But what's the result of these two rule sets? Well, the border will become 3px wide (the default border width for a visible border,) and it'll be colored green, not blue. This happens because the second rule set uses shorthand to define the border-style as solid, but doesn't define the other two properties (border-width and border-color).

This might sound a bit complicated at first, but it's worth experimenting with to get the hang of it. Just understand that if you don't define all the properties represented in a shorthand property, the missing ones will revert to their defaults, rather than inheriting from any existing styles.

In most cases, this won't cause too many problems, but in some instances (for example, when using the font shorthand property) it could have undesirable and confusing results, as described in an article on my site.[1]

---

[1] http://www.impressivewebs.com/a-primer-on-the-css-font-shorthand-property/

Another thing to understand about shorthand is that for certain shorthand properties, the missing values are inherited based on the existing values. Two good examples, which you'll often use in this way, are `margin` and `padding`. For example:

```
.box {
  padding: 20px 10px 15px;
}
```

Notice there are three values specified. If you recall from Chapter 1, these values represent padding for the top, right, bottom, and left, in that order. The fourth value (referencing the left padding) is missing, but it is assumed to be 10px, which matches the opposite side padding (the second value declared). If we had omitted two values, then the bottom would inherit from the top in addition to the left inheriting from the right.

The same principle applies to other shorthand properties like `margin`, `border-color`, and `border-width`. So the following two lines of code would yield the exact same results:

```
.example {
  margin: 10px 20px 10px 20px;
}

.example {
  margin: 10px 20px;
}
```

In the first declaration, we're defining all four margin values explicitly (`top`, `right`, `bottom`, and `left`). In the second declaration, we're omitting the `bottom` and `left`, so they'll inherit from the `top` and `right` values. In the same way, the following two examples would also produce the same result:

```
.example {
  border-width: 10px 10px 10px 10px;
}

.example {
  border-width: 10px;
}
```

Again, we're defining all four explicitly in the first declaration, but in the second declaration, we're letting the missing values inherit from the only value that's defined: the top value for the border width.

Using shorthand in this way is a good habit to pick up early because it'll help you to omit unnecessary stuff in your code, making it easier to read.

Float-based Layouts

The first layout technique that we're going to discuss is the only current example that works in every browser and doesn't use HTML tables (tables are not good for layout[2]). There are a number of new techniques that we'll touch on later in the chapter that are supported in some modern browsers, but float-based layouts are still necessary for websites that need to look good in older browsers like Internet Explorer versions 7, 8, and 9. Even modern browsers have sketchy support for newer layout methods so, at the time of writing, float-based layouts are the primary layout method used in CSS.

In our RecipeFinder website, we have an ideal place to use a float-based layout: the main content area. This area is divided into two vertical columns, as shown in Figure 2.3:

---

[2] http://stackoverflow.com/questions/83073/why-not-use-tables-for-layout-in-html

Figure 2.3. The two-column area of RecipeFinder

Let's add some layout styles to that section of code, so we can get things started:

```
.main {
  width: 1020px;
  margin: 0 auto;
}

  .latest {
    width: 640px;
    float: left;
  }

  .sidebar {
```

```
    width: 360px;
    float: right;
}
```

You'll recognize these selectors from Chapter 1, where we introduced the bare CSS. The HTML that this applies to includes the `.main` element, which wraps both columns. You'll notice we've applied a margin declaration to `.main`.

As discussed earlier, this margin declaration is shorthand and would be equivalent to the following:

```
.main {
    margin: 0 auto 0 auto;
}
```

But we've omitted the final two values for brevity, as they're inherited from the existing values. While the zero values are probably easy to figure out (they declare that no margins should exist on the top and bottom of the `.main` element), the `auto` values will be new to you.

A value of `auto` set on the left and right margins of an element that has an explicitly defined width, will automatically center that element horizontally inside its parent. It won't center the contents of the element; only the element itself. In the case of the `.main` element, its parent is the `<body>` element, which has no set width. So whatever the horizontal size (or width,) of the browser, the `.main` element will center itself horizontally on the page as a result of this margin declaration.

That's a CSS technique that you'll want to tattoo on the back of your hand—you'll use it often. But it only works with horizontal centering. Vertical centering is a trickier thing to accomplish in CSS.[3]

 CSS Units

> You'll notice that throughout the examples, numerical values are appended with "px." This refers to pixels and is just one kind of CSS unit. Other commonly used units include percentages (%), ems, and rems. We'll discuss more CSS units in the next chapter.

---

[3] http://blog.themeforest.net/tutorials/vertical-centering-with-css/

Next in our CSS, we have the two elements inside the .main element. The first is the left column, which has a class of .latest (referring to the "latest recipes"). The other column is an <aside> element to which we've applied a class of .sidebar.

As discussed earlier in the section covering block and inline elements, since both of these elements are block-level, they will, by default, appear one after the other, stacked vertically, rather than side-by-side filling the available horizontal space of their parent element—which, in this case is the .main element.

To have them appear side by side in a two-column format, we use the float property, which tells the browser to push the element towards a specified side of the page, as far as it can go. The float property can accept one of three values: none, left, or right.

To achieve the effect we want, we apply float: left to the left column, and float: right to the right column. In addition, the specified widths help balance the columns so they match how they look in the Photoshop mock-up.

At this stage, with all our content in place, the content inside the .main element should look like Figure 2.4.

Latest Recipes

Zesty Smoked Haddock Skewers

Cooking time: 20 minutes

Creamy Blueberry Bagel

Cooking time: 7 minutes

Traditional Roast Beef with Yorkshire Sauce

Cooking time: 50 minutes

Most Popular

4.9/5
Delicious baked garlic bread
4.8/5
Chocolate cloud cake
4.8/5
Fiery Thai curry
4.7/5
Sensational portobello mushrooms stuffed with stilton
4.6/5
Crab, corn and potato cake
4.3/5
Persian style lamb pilaf

Yummy Tweets

@Peter   Once again, the recipe of the aussie BBQ was a complete success thx @RecipeFinder
24 minutes ago

@xavier_mathieu : I love the recipe "Cuisses de grenouilles" so much
1 hour ago

@UncleBens : Easy to cook and so good to eat: the creamy raspberry bagel via @RecipeFinder
2 days ago

@RecipeFinder : Thanks folks for all the love in your messages
2 days ago

Recipe Categories

- Meat free recipes
- Thai recipes
- Dairy free recipes
- French recipes
- Vegan recipes
- Aussie recipes
- Shellfish-free recipes
- Children recipes

Our Contributors

Figure 2.4. Our two columns after adding the float property

Pretty bland, isn't it? We haven't added many styles yet, so what we see is mostly what's left as a result of our **Normalize.css** file, along with some browser defaults (like blue text links).

Clearing Floats

This next concept, "clearing floats," is something you'll have to deal with in almost all float-based layouts. To illustrate why we need to do this, let's add two new temporary declarations to our .main element, which is the element that contains our "floated" columns:

```
.main {
  width: 1020px;
  margin: 0 auto 0 auto;
```

```
  outline: solid 1px red;
  background: green;
}
```

The last two declarations are only temporary styles, to illustrate a point. Figure 2.5 shows what happens when those styles are added to the CSS and the page is refreshed.

Latest Recipes

Zesty Smoked Haddock Skewers

Cooking time: 20 minutes

Creamy Blueberry Bagel

Cooking time: 7 minutes

Traditional Roast Beef with Yorkshire Sauce

Cooking time: 50 minutes

Most Popular

4.9/5
Delicious baked garlic bread
4.8/5
Chocolate cloud cake
4.8/5
Fiery Thai curry
4.7/5
Sensational portobello mushrooms stuffed with stilton
4.6/5
Crab, corn and potato cake
4.3/5
Persian style lamb pilaf

Yummy Tweets

@Peter : Once again, the recipe of the aussie BBQ was a complete success thx @RecipeFinder
24 minutes ago

@xavier_mathieu : I love the recipe "Cuisses de grenouilles" so much
1 hour ago

@UncleBens : Easy to cook and so good to eat: the creamy raspberry bagel via @RecipeFinder
2 days ago

@RecipeFinder Thanks folks for all the love in your messages
2 days ago

Recipe Categories

- Meat free recipes
- Thai recipes
- Dairy free recipes
- French recipes
- Vegan recipes
- Aussie recipes
- Shellfish-free recipes
- Children recipes

Figure 2.5. The floated columns cause the container to collapse

What we might normally expect to happen here is that the background appear green and a full red outline appear around all the contents of the `.main` element. But all we see is a 2px horizontal line at the top of the `.main` element.

This happens because of the floated child elements. When one or more elements are floated, unless other non-floated elements are present, the parent element of the floats will effectively collapse, behaving like there's nothing inside it. All that needs to be done is remove one of the float declarations, and the full green background and red outline will appear as expected.

So in order to remedy the situation, floats need to be "cleared." We can do this by adding a new section of code to our **styles.css** file:

```css
.cf:before,
.cf:after {
    content: " ";
    display: table;
}

.cf:after {
    clear: both;
}

.cf {
    *zoom: 1; /* for IE6 and IE7 */
}
```

This float clearing method (often referred to as a "clearfix," hence the cf class selector,) comes again via Nicolas Gallagher.[4] Don't be intimidated by what you see here; you don't have to understand everything in this chunk of code. Once we have this in our stylesheet we just need to add a class of cf to any element that collapses due to floats.

Notice this fix uses pseudo-elements (which we briefly introduced in Chapter 1,) and a couple of new properties, including the clear property.

The clear property prevents an element from being affected by floated elements that appear before it. Floats generally cause all other elements to wrap around them, making them bump up against the side opposite the float direction. But adding the clear property to subsequent elements causes those elements to drop below the floated element, just as they would if there were no floats present.

To cause the new styles to apply to our layout, let's add a new class to our .main element:

```html
<div class="main cf">
```

---

[4] http://nicolasgallagher.com/micro-clearfix-hack/

Notice the space separating the two classes. This is one of the features briefly mentioned in Chapter 1 that makes classes a far superior selector in comparison to other options: the fact that you can use multiple classes on a single HTML element.

With those styles in place, the green background and red outline will appear as expected, confirming that our floated elements are now "clear." We can then remove the background and outline we added.

Another benefit of clearing the floats is that our footer content is now appearing below the .main content, where it should be (albeit still unstyled) instead of bumping up against the right side of the left column as it was prior to adding the clearfix. It's worth noting that we could have caused the footer to drop below the .main element's content simply by adding "clear: both" to the footer element itself. However, this would not have fixed the float clearing problem where the .main element was collapsing.

Positioning in CSS

Another useful layout technique involves the use of CSS's position property. Although it's possible to use this technique for layouts, in most cases you wouldn't use it for large structural elements the way you would with floats. Positioning, however, can come in handy to help place or align a specific element in a very precise manner.

A good candidate for this technique is the bottom half of our sidebar, the section called "Yummy Tweets," shown in Figure 2.6.

Figure 2.6. Our Yummy Tweets, as they appear in our original design

We're going to use the `position` property to place the Twitter icons that you see next to each of those tweets. But before we do this, let's consider exactly what properties we'll use and how they work.

Absolute and Relative Positioning

CSS allows us to place an element anywhere on a page using the `top`, `bottom`, `left`, and `right` properties along with the `position` property. Let's look at an example:

```css
.example {
  position: absolute;
  top: 100px;
  left: 150px;
}
```

If there are no other positioning-related styles on our page, the `.example` element shown above would be positioned 100px from the top and 100px from the left of the browser window (also called the **viewport**).

But this isn't very practical. It's not often that you'll want to position an element relative to the browser window like this. The real practical value of absolute positioning comes from combining it with a positioned parent element. Let's improve on the code we just wrote and demonstrate what's meant by "positioned parent":

```css
.wrapper {
  position: relative;
}

.example {
  position: absolute;
  top: 100px;
  left: 150px;
}
```

Now, instead of positioning the element relative to the full browser window, we're forcing positioning to occur relative to the `.wrapper` element. The relative positioning set on `.wrapper` creates a **positioning context** for any positioned child elements.

Now let's combine this technique with the pseudo-elements we introduced in Chapter 1, so we can position our Twitter icon next to each tweet in our sidebar. Here is the HTML for a single "Yummy Tweet":

```html
<div class="tweet">
    <p><a href="#">@Peter</a> : Once again, the recipe of the Aussie
➥BBQ was a complete success thx <a href="#">@RecipeFinder</a><br>
    <a href="#" class="date">24 minutes ago</a></p>
</div>
```

We're going to target the outer `<div>` element that has a class of `tweet` using the following CSS:

```css
.tweet {
  padding-left: 55px;
  padding-right: 20px;
  position: relative;
}
```

```
.tweet:before {
  content: url(../images/twitter-icon.png);
  display: block;
  position: absolute;
  left: 15px;
  top: 4px;
}
```

A pseudo-element uses the single-colon or double-colon syntax (we're using single-colon for better browser support[5]) in combination with another CSS selector, to add a phony (i.e. "pseudo") element inside the targeted element (the .tweet element). In this example, we're using a before pseudo-element, so the inserted element will appear before the .tweet element's content.

Notice that the .tweet element is positioned relatively. Also notice that there are 55 pixels of padding set on the left side of the .tweet element. Next, in the pseudo-element selector, we're using the content property to define what exactly we want to insert (in this case it's a transparent PNG Twitter icon,) and then we're positioning the pseudo-element absolutely, 4px from the top and 40px from the left.

If we wanted, we could have inserted the Twitter icon inside our HTML using an <img> tag. But in this case, since the icons are just decoration, we have the option to use a pseudo-element or background image. By contrast, the images that appear in the "Latest Recipes" section are not just decoration but are part of the main content; so those shouldn't be inserted as background images or pseudo-elements via CSS, but should be placed into the HTML using <img> tags. We'll talk more about backgrounds in the next chapter.

Since our pseudo-element is placed on the page using a class selector of .tweet, the pseudo-element will appear on every element on the page that has a class of tweet. After we add these styles and refresh the page, our Yummy Tweets section will look like Figure 2.7.

---

[5] http://www.impressivewebs.com/before-after-css3/

Yummy Tweets

@Peter : Once again, the recipe of the Aussie BBQ was a complete success thx @RecipeFinder
24 minutes ago

@xavier_mathieu : I love the recipe "Cuisses de grenouilles" so much
1 hour ago

@UncleBens : Easy to cook and so good to eat: the creamy raspberry bagel via @RecipeFinder
2 days ago

@RecipeFinder : Thanks folks for all the love in your messages
2 days ago

Figure 2.7. Our Yummy Tweets after adding the Twitter icons using pseudo-elements

Adding the pseudo-element using absolute positioning is just one step towards styling this area. Overall, our website still needs a lot of styling, as does the Yummy Tweets section.

What about Responsive Web Design?

One of the biggest trends in the web design industry right now is Responsive Web Design (RWD). This book is an introduction to CSS, so we won't be covering that particular technique in exhaustive detail; however, I will introduce the topic here, and in Chapter 5 we'll use responsive design techniques to complete the coding of RecipeFinder.

So what exactly is responsive design? Briefly, it involves coding the CSS in such a way that it ensures the width of the website and its content adapt to the size of the user's browser window. This means if the user visits on a desktop PC browser at 1920x1080 resolution or a cellphone at 320x480, the content and layout will adjust to fit.

RWD is centered on the use of media queries, a CSS feature that we haven't discussed yet. Let's take a quick look at the syntax for media queries so you can see how they can be used to build a responsive web design:

```
@media (max-width: 1500px) {

}

@media (max-width: 1200px) {

}

@media (max-width: 900px) {

}
```

What you see above are referred to in CSS as **at-rules**. There are other at-rules (identified by the @ symbol,) such as the `@font-face` rule, which we'll talk about in Chapter 4.

The `@media` at-rules are used to define different CSS styles depending on certain media features, such as the width of the browser window. Inside the `@media` blocks, (each of which starts and ends with the opening and closing curly braces,) you can include full rule sets. You can even repeat certain rule sets in separate media query blocks in order to override existing styles.

In Chapter 5, once we have the bulk of the site done, we'll add some custom media queries to make the RecipeFinder website responsive.

Using `box-sizing` for Intuitive Sizing

Normally, when an element is given a specified width—for example, our `.main` element has a width of 1020px—if you add left or right padding to that element, the width of the element would increase by the amount of left and right padding that was added. Look at the following example:

```
.box {
   width: 400px;
   padding-left: 20px;
   padding-right: 20px;
}
```

Although the width of the `.box` element is defined explicitly as 400px, the actual width of the element will end up being 440px, because the left and right padding add to the width.

For a long time this has been an irritation that we've learned to deal with in CSS layouts. With the `box-sizing` property, however, we can tell the browser to render all of our widths and heights at an exact pixel size, including any borders or padding settings. That is, if we define an explicit width or height, padding and borders will not affect that width and height.

We're going to add this property to the top of our custom styles, using the universal selector:

```
* {
 -webkit-box-sizing: border-box;
 -moz-box-sizing: border-box;
 box-sizing: border-box;
}
```

The three lines of code you see here are exactly the same, but because some browsers' support for these properties is "experimental," we're forced to use vendor prefixes (the `-webkit-` and `-moz-` prefixes in this example) for maximum browser compatibility. We'll talk more about vendor prefixes in Chapter 5.

With this declaration in place, we can feel free to add padding and/or borders to any elements, and we won't have to recalculate their specified widths for them to lay out correctly. Let's do that now by adding some padding to the `.latest` element (which is our left column):

```
.latest {
   width: 640px;
   float: left;
   padding: 0 40px;
}
```

If we had added this padding prior to adding the box-sizing declarations, the left column would no longer fit next to the right column inside of .main. But, by using box-sizing, we prevent the padding from adding to the overall width of the column.

Adding More Layout Styles

We've already sized and centered the .main element. If you've been following along with the code examples, you'll notice, however, that the header, promo (which is the big photo below the header), and footer sections are not aligned with the .main element. So, let's align those now:

```css
.header-inside {
  width: 1020px;
  margin: 0 auto;
}

.promo {
  width: 1020px;
  margin: 0 auto;
}

.footer-inside {
  width: 1020px;
  margin: 0 auto;
}
```

First, to help with the look we're trying to achieve, we've added an inner element inside our <header> and <footer> elements. Those two new elements in the HTML are classed as .header-inside and .footer-inside, respectively. We're doing this so we can center the content inside the header and footer, while allowing the background of those elements to expand horizontally to the edges of the browser window.

You can see this demonstrated in Figure 2.8.

Figure 2.8. The footer has a set width, but the background color expands to the full width of the window

Here you can see that, although the width of the footer area has expanded to the left and right (mimicking what might happen on a wider browser window), the content itself stays centered. The extra element inside `<footer>` helps achieve this.

There's a problem, though. The styles in each of these three declaration blocks (`.header-inside`, `.promo`, and `.footer-inside`) are exactly the same, and they even match the styles we added to the `.main` element. Here's an opportunity for us to take these common styles and create a simple reusable class that we can apply to any element that needs these exact styles.

So instead of four separate rule sets with the same styles, we'll have one rule set as follows:

```css
.center-global {
  width: 1020px;
  margin: 0 auto;
}
```

And then we'll add that class to every HTML element that needs those styles. Because of this reusable class we've created, we'll no longer need the `.header-inside` class, so we'll remove that from our HTML and CSS. The `.promo` and `.footer-inside` classes will be used later, so we'll keep those.

Floating the "Latest Recipes" Images

We've already used the `float` property to help build our primary two-column layout. Next, we'll use the same property for its intended purpose: to allow text and inline content to flow around a floated block element. In our HTML, we have a simple structure for each of the entries added in our "Latest Recipes" section:

```
<div class="media">

    <a href="#">
        <img src="images/haddock.jpg" alt="Haddock skewers">
        <h2>Zesty Smoked Haddock Skewers</h2>
        <p>Cooking time: 20 minutes</p>
    </a>

</div>
```

Currently, the <h2> and <p> elements in each of these .media sections are appearing below the image in the .media section. You'll remember from our discussion of block versus inline elements that this happens because all block elements will naturally drop below other elements placed before them in the markup. We can override this behavior using float and clear:

```
.media {
  clear: left;
  padding-bottom: 28px;
}

  .media img {
    float: left;
    margin-right: 30px;
  }
```

Here we've floated the image left, which causes the text content to bump up against it. We also need to clear the .media element to ensure that it doesn't get affected by the floated images.

We've also added a right margin to the image and bottom padding to the .media element to match what's in the design mockup. However, you'll notice when you apply these styles that the padding at the bottom of the .media element doesn't seem to appear, as shown in Figure 2.9.

Latest Recipes

Zesty Smoked Haddock Skewers

Cooking time: 20 minutes

Creamy Blueberry Bagel

Cooking time: 7 minutes

Traditional Roast Beef with Yorkshire Sauce

Cooking time: 50 minutes

Figure 2.9. Our .media images floated left, but the bottom padding has failed to take effect

This is due to the `float` property. As discussed earlier in the section on clearing floats, a parent element will expand vertically to contain only content that is non-floated. To fix this, we would need to add our `cf` class to all the `.media` elements.

Unfortunately, doing this would add a lot of extra HTML that, in this instance, isn't necessary. So to clear the floats here, we're going to use a different method—the `overflow` property set to a value of `"hidden"`:

```
.media {
  clear: left;
  padding-bottom: 28px;
  overflow: hidden;
}
```

This is a simple float-clearing method that you'll want to keep in mind for smaller elements like these. For larger layout-related elements, it's almost always better to go with the full-blown clearfix I introduced earlier. But in this case, we're better off using `overflow: hidden`.[6] With this declaration in place, the padding at the bottom of each `.media` element will take effect.

Layout Styles for the Header

Now that we have our "Latest Recipes" section laid out correctly, we have two final areas of our site to which we want to add some layout styles: the header and footer.

Let's start with the header content, along with the navigation links. Here's the HTML for our `<header>` section:

```
<header>

    <div class="center-global cf">

        <a href="#"><img src="images/logo.png" alt="RecipeFinder
➥logo" class="logo"></a>

        <nav>
            <ul>
                <li><a href="#">Recipes</a></li>
                <li><a href="#">Ingredients</a></li>
                <li><a href="#">Contributors</a></li>
            </ul>
        </nav>

    </div>

</header>
```

Notice the unordered list (`<ul>`) that holds our navigation links. Now let's add some CSS:

```
.logo {
  float: left;
  margin-left: 145px;
  margin-top: -34px;
  position: relative;
  top: 34px;
```

---

[6] For a discussion of the different methods to clear floats, and why `overflow: hidden` can cause problems, see http://www.impressivewebs.com/clearing-floats-why-necessary/.

```
}

nav {
    float: right;
    margin-right: 177px;
    padding-top: 20px;
}

    nav ul {
        list-style: none;
        margin: 0;
        padding: 0;
    }

        nav ul li {
            display: inline-block;
            *display: inline; /* for IE7 */
            margin-right: 30px;
        }
```

There's a lot going on here, some of which you'll recognize from earlier in the book, but let's break down the new bits of code.

First, we're using relative positioning along with the top property to push our .logo element down from its original position. Relative positioning used in this way moves an element but allows the original space it occupies to remain intact. We're doing this so that the bottom edge of the logo will overlap the .promo section, which is what the design in our Photoshop mockup requires.

We're also floating the logo left and floating the navigation section to the right and aligning these using margins and padding. Next we have the <ul> element along with its child <li> elements. The list-style property, which we apply to the <ul>, is a shorthand property that defines the type of bullet we want to have on the list (the default value is "disc"), along with the position of the bullet. We've added a value of "none" to the list and we've set the margins and padding on the list to zero values, overriding the browser defaults for these.

Finally, in order to get the list items to align horizontally, we've set the list items to display: inline-block, and we've added a hack (the repeated style with the asterisk character[7]) to get this to work in IE7. Figure 2.10 shows how the header will look after we've added these styles.

Figure 2.10. Our header and navigation links after adding some layout styles

Laying out the Promo Photo

For the big promo photo that appears below the logo and navigation, there isn't too much to do except get the photo description and "cook it now!" button to appear overlaid on top of the big image.

Here's the HTML for our promo section:

```
<div class="promo center-global">

    <img src="images/promo.jpg" alt="Zucchini Puree">

    <div class="promo-desc">
    <h1>Sweet and Sour Zucchini Puree</h1>
    <a href="#" class="promo-btn">cook it now!</a>
    </div>

</div>
```

Take note of the <div> with a class of .promo-desc that wraps our <h1> element and the link below it. We're going to add some absolute positioning to the .promo-desc element to place it over the promo image. Here's the CSS:

```
.promo {
  position: relative;
}

.promo-desc {
  position: absolute;
```

[7] http://www.impressivewebs.com/ie7-ie8-css-hacks/

```
    bottom: 93px;
    right: 75px;
}
```

You'll remember this technique from earlier in the chapter. The `.promo` element creates a positioning context when we add relative positioning to it. With that in place, any absolutely positioned elements inside of it will be positioned relative to it (that is, to the `.promo` element). But hold on a second! Figure 2.11 shows what happens when we add these styles.

Figure 2.11. The logo is partially hidden after adding relative positioning to the promo section

Notice in Figure 2.11 that our text and link are placed roughly where we want them, but that the bottom of our logo, which we carefully positioned earlier in this chapter, is now overlapped by the big promo image. We won't get into all the gory technical details on what's causing this, but, to put it briefly, it's happening because of the relative positioning we've added to the elements. But never fear! We can fix this with a few additions to our `.logo` and `.promo` rule sets:

```
.logo {
  float: left;
  margin-left: 145px;
  margin-top: -34px;
  position: relative;
  top: 34px;
  z-index: 10;
}

.promo {
```

```
    position: relative;
    z-index: 5;
}
```

Here we've added the z-index property to help adjust the stacking of these elements. The z-index property accepts an integer value and will only work on elements that are explicitly positioned using the position property. z-index adjusts the position of elements in relation to one another along the z axis. This means instead of moving elements from left to right or top to bottom, we're moving them forwards or backwards.

And so, if you're looking directly at a browser window, a higher z-index value means the element will be (in a manner of speaking,) closer to you; whereas a lower z-index value will push the element further away from you.

But, as mentioned, this will only happen in relation to other positioned elements, and will not work for non-positioned elements. This is an important point to keep in mind when using z-index, as this will often trip up CSS beginners.[8]

So in our example, we've set the z-index property to "10" on the .logo element and "5" on the .promo element, which fixes the problem, as shown in Figure 2.12.

Figure 2.12. The logo overlap problem corrected using z-index

Laying out the Footer

The next thing we'll do to our RecipeFinder site in terms of layout is get the contents of our footer aligned. Our footer is made up of three sections: "Recipes Categories,"

---

[8] http://coding.smashingmagazine.com/2009/09/15/the-z-index-css-property-a-comprehensive-look/

"Our Contributors," and "Colophon." Each of these sections is wrapped in its own separate <div> element, with its contents in an unordered list (<ul>).

We'll again use our handy `float` property, this time to create a three-column layout:

```
.footer-1 {
  float: left;
  width: 422px;
}

.footer-2 {
  float: left;
  width: 326px;
}

.footer-3 {
  float: left;
  width: 232px;
}
```

We'll also add a little padding to the left side of the `.footer-inside` element, which holds the three footer sections:

```
.footer-inside {
  padding-left: 40px;
}
```

This aligns the left side of the footer content with the content above it. Figure 2.13 shows how our footer will look after we add these layout styles.

Figure 2.13. Our footer after adding floats and widths to the three sections inside the footer

Laying out the "Most Popular" Recipes

Finally, we have one more layout-related issue to work out—specifically the section in our sidebar called "Most Popular." We're again going to incorporate floats to deal with this. Figure 2.14 shows what this section looks like in our original design.

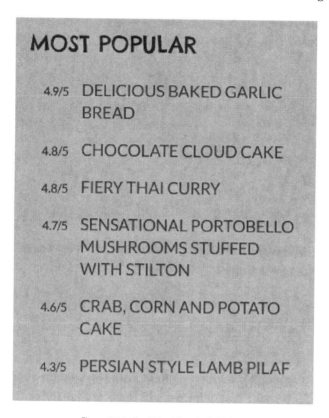

Figure 2.14. Our "Most Popular" sidebar

Below the heading we have recipe ratings in a left column, and the recipe names in a right column. Here's what our HTML looks like for an individual recipe/rating pair:

```
<div class="rating">4.9/5</div>
<div class="pop-item"><a href="#">Delicious garlic bread</a></div>
```

This would be repeated for each recipe, with the content changed to reflect each one. Now let's add some CSS to style these elements:

```
.rating {
  float: left;
  clear: left;
  padding-top: 4px;
  padding-right: 15px;
  width: 45px;
}

.pop-item {
  padding-bottom: 20px;
  float: left;
  width: 250px;
}
```

All of the properties here are ones we've used or discussed earlier in the book. The .rating elements are all floated to the left, and each of these is also cleared. This prevents any of the .rating element from bumping up against the .pop-item elements. The .pop-item elements are also floated left, but they're not cleared. As we learned earlier, clearing pushes the cleared element to a new line, which we don't want to happen to the .pop-item elements. However, we *do* want that to happen to the .rating elements. Both elements are given a set width, and we've added some padding to match what's in the design.

The last thing we need to add to this section is a wrapper <div> with a class of popular holding all these ratings and recipes together. We'll add some padding to the bottom of this element, to help keep it separate from the Yummy Tweets section below it:

```
.popular {
  padding-bottom: 40px;
}
```

What's the future of CSS Layouts?

What we've done in this chapter is use a tried-and-true, cross-browser method for laying out pages with CSS—namely, using floats. But, as alluded to earlier, the float property was not created for this purpose (although we're certainly thankful that it works fairly well).

For this reason, the newest browsers have started adding support for CSS layout features that we hope to be using exclusively in a few years (assuming older browsers that don't auto-update, like IE8 and IE9, die out).

We won't discuss these new layout features in detail here, because those features are still in flux and browser support isn't as good as we'd like it to be. But we will list some of those new layout techniques along with links so you can access articles, tutorials, and tools to help you learn these new features.

Flexbox

Flexbox has the most browser support of any new CSS layout feature. If you're going to study any new layout feature as an alternative to floats, start with this one. Unfortunately, the syntax for Flexbox has changed a few times. Below are some resources to help get you up to speed:

Dive into Flexbox	http://weblog.bocoup.com/dive-into-flexbox/
An Introduction to the CSS Flexbox Module	http://net.tutsplus.com/tutorials/html-css-techniques/an-introduction-to-css-flexbox/
"Old" Flexbox and "New" Flexbox	http://css-tricks.com/old-flexbox-and-new-flexbox/
CSS Flexbox Please!	http://demo.agektmr.com/flexbox/

Other New Layout Features

Other new layout techniques are much further away from common use, but below are some official specifications for techniques you might want to keep an eye on:

CSS Regions	http://dev.w3.org/csswg/css3-regions/
CSS Exclusions and Shapes	http://dev.w3.org/csswg/css3-exclusions/
Grid Template Layout and Grid Layout	http://dev.w3.org/csswg/css3-layout/
	http://dev.w3.org/csswg/css3-grid-layout/

Many of these techniques and more are discussed in Peter Gasston's article for .*net* magazine.[9] For beginners, the official specifications will probably be too much for

---

[9] http://www.netmagazine.com/features/future-css-layouts

you to handle. But at least take a quick look so you can get familiar with features that will slowly start gaining wider browser support.

Summary

The layout for each section of our website is now in place. We've covered a lot of ground here, including a quick intro to the box model, the difference between block and inline elements, float-based layouts, positioning, and a brief look at responsive design.

By now you'll be keen to see some color and style added to our page. In the next two chapters we'll learn a whole slew of CSS features that will really perk up our sample website.

Chapter 3

Backgrounds, Borders, and More

If you've started to build the sample website, you'll have noticed that, although we have the major sections of our page laid out, it's not looking much like the original Photoshop mockup just yet.

Figure 3.1 shows you what our page looks like right now. With our basic layout in place, let's learn how we can spruce up our page visually so it'll be more appealing, and reflect what we have in our original design.

Figure 3.1. RecipeFinder after the layout styles from Chapter 2

Backgrounds

The first thing we want to take care of in this chapter is the primary background that sits behind a large portion of RecipeFinder. Figure 3.2 shows a close-up of the area behind the "Latest Recipes" section, as shown in our original Photoshop file.

Figure 3.2. A close-up view of the RecipeFinder background

This is zoomed in so we can see that not only is the background a light creamy brown color, but it's also overlaid with a subtle texture. This texture, along with the color that it overlays, will be placed onto our page as a background image. Let's look at the code we're going to use to do this:

```
body {
  background: #cab5a3 url(../images/bg-main.gif) repeat repeat 0 0;
}
```

The first point to note in this example is the selector we're using: body. This tells the browser that the declaration block will apply to the <body> element (which is the next element down from the <html> element in our HTML hierarchy).

Next, you'll notice that we're using the background property, which is a shorthand property. We learned about shorthand in Chapter 2. This particular example helps us define a number of different background-related properties using a single line of code. If we didn't use shorthand, this single declaration would look like this:

```
body {
  background-color: #cab5a3;
  background-image: url(../images/bg-main.gif);
  background-repeat: repeat repeat;
  background-position: 0 0;
}
```

This would give us exactly the same result as the single-line version. You'll be using the properties described here regularly in future projects, so let's discuss each of them in detail.

First, we've defined a background color for the <body>. This is good practice as it ensures that the user will see something similar to the background image should it fail to load quickly enough, or at all. Also, if the background image is dark, say, with light-colored text, this will ensure readability. In this case, we're using a color value of #cab5a3—more on color values later in this chapter. This color was arrived at simply by sampling part of the textured background in the Photoshop file, and then copying and pasting the color value from Photoshop into my CSS file.

Next, we have the declaration that tells the browser what background image to use on the <body> element. The syntax uses the url() notation to reference the background image. This is the syntax you'll use most often when including an image in a web page using CSS. The path to the file needs to be relative to the location of the CSS file, which is why, in this case, we're using "../" at the start of the path. This tells the browser that the background image is located up one level in the folder structure (represented by "..") and inside a folder called "**images**" (represented by "/images").

This background image file is a GIF file that has an original size of 129px by 129px. So how does such a small image fill the background? This brings us to the next background-related property in our rule set.

The background-repeat property is used to define whether we want the background to appear only once, or if we want it to repeat vertically, horizontally, or both. For the <body> element, we want the background to repeat throughout the entire <body>, so we set the value to repeat repeat. Alternatively, we could write repeat just once, which would have the same result, because it would assume the missing second value is the same as the first. I've included both values explicitly to demonstrate that you can have two different values defined. The first value represents horizontal repeat, and the second value represents vertical.

Other commonly used values for background repeat are no-repeat (meaning we don't want it to repeat), repeat-x (which repeats the image horizontally, or along the x axis,) and repeat-y (which repeats the image vertically, or along the y axis).

When using the *x* and *y* repeat values, you only need to define one, as the other is assumed to be no-repeat.

Finally, the last line in the code uses the background-position property. This will accept any pair of unit values, separated by a space. You can use pixels, ems, percentages, and more—we'll discuss values and units in more detail later in this chapter. This property tells the browser where to position the background image. In our example, we haven't needed to define this value (the default is "0 0", which is what we're using), but it's been included for reference, as it's a property you'll employ often.

The background-position property will work only if you're using no-repeat on at least one of the directions (horizontal or vertical) in the background-repeat property. The background position tells the browser where to place the background when it starts to repeat, relative to the element on which the background is applied. For example, a non-repeating background with a background-position property set to "30px 40px" will position the background 30 pixels from the left and 40 pixels from the top of the element on which it's applied. You also have the option to use keywords like top, left, center, right, and bottom.

Some of this might sound confusing on first read, but I encourage you to play around with the values for all these properties to see the results of different combinations. Experimenting is the best way to familiarize yourself with the subtleties of each value combination, and this applies not only to backgrounds, but also to any complex CSS feature. You'll often use backgrounds in CSS, so it's worth taking the time to get to know this shorthand property and its longhand equivalents.

With this background in place, we now have some color in the RecipeFinder website (besides the color photos, that is).

Borders

In our Photoshop file, in the "Latest Recipes" section on the left side of our sample website, each image has a thick border—something that's currently missing in our coded version.

Figure 3.3. The "Latest Recipes" images in our design have borders

To add the border, we'll use the border property, appending that to the existing styles on the <img> elements, which are targeted in our CSS as children of the .media element:

```
.media img {
  float: left;
  margin-right: 30px;
  border: solid 9px #ede0d5;
}
```

Here we're using the border shorthand property to define the following three properties on a single line:

- border-style, which accepts a number of keyword values like dotted, dashed, and inset
- border-width, which accepts a unit value
- border-color, which accepts any valid CSS color value

For many shorthand properties, you can rearrange the values and the result would be the same. But some shorthand properties require a specific order—for example, the font property.

Figure 3.4 shows us what our "Latest Recipes" section will look like after adding the border.

Figure 3.4. The "Latest Recipes" images with borders added

Rounded Corners

While we're fixing up the images in the "Latest Recipes" section, let's discuss how we can easily add rounded corners to any element on the page. This is a technique that has, for a long time, been carried out using images, extra HTML, JavaScript, and other overly complex techniques.

For the RecipeFinder website, we won't need to add any rounded corners to our design, so we'll use this as a temporary demonstration only. If we did want to add rounded corners to each image, we could do so like this:

```
.media img {
  float: left;
  margin-right: 30px;
```

```
  border: solid 9px #ede0d5;
  border-radius: 20%;
}
```

And this would have the effect shown in Figure 3.5.

Figure 3.5. It's easy to add rounded corners with CSS

Notice the new property being used: `border-radius`. The `border-radius` property is a shorthand property that can accept up to four values. The values represent (in order,) the `top-left`, `top-right`, `bottom-right`, and `bottom-left` corners. As is the case with any shorthand properties that use unit values, any omitted values are inherited from existing ones. See the section in Chapter 2 on shorthand for a review of how this works.

You can explicitly target individual corners of an element using the longhand syntax. For example, the following would be equivalent to the `border-radius` declaration that we just used:

```
.media img {
  border-top-left-radius: 20%;
  border-top-right-radius: 20%;
```

```
    border-bottom-right-radius: 20%;
    border-bottom-left-radius: 20%;
}
```

You can see clearly why, in most cases, you'll use the shorthand syntax. Even if you want to target a single corner, it's much more efficient to do this instead:

```
.media img {
    border-radius: 20% 0 0 0;
}
```

As mentioned above, our original design doesn't use any rounded corners, so we won't employ this technique here. That said, it's a good weapon to have in your arsenal.

Values and Units

So far in the book, we've used a number of different types of values and units. Some have been straightforward while others may have looked confusing at first glance. Since values and units are an important part of CSS, it's a good time to pause here and explore this topic in a little more depth.

Probably the simplest way to understand these concepts is to see some examples of the most common types of values and units, along with brief description of each. In these examples, don't worry too much about the parts of the code you don't yet understand; just focus on the parts being discussed.

Px Units

We've come across the px, or pixels, unit of measurement many times already. It represents tiny squares that make up all elements on a web page:

```
.example {
    width: 200px;
}
```

To see what I'm referring to, Figure 3.6 shows a screenshot of part of the RecipeFinder logo, but zoomed in 1600% in Photoshop.

Figure 3.6. The RecipeFinder logo zoomed in to show the pixels

At this magnification it's easy to see that the logo is made up entirely of those tiny squares, or pixels. Pixels are the most common type of unit you see in CSS.

Em Units

The em unit is a little complicated to grasp at first, but once you get the hang of it, it's very useful:

```
.example {
  padding: 10em;
}
```

A single em is always equal to whatever the value is of the `font-size` property on the element to which the em unit is applied. The `font-size` property defines the size of the font, or text, on the element. Take the following example HTML:

```
<div class="box">
  <p>Let's em-phasize this point.</p>
</div>
```

And here's the accompanying CSS:

```
.box {
  font-size: 20px;
  padding: 1.5em;
}

p {
  font-size: 14px;
  padding: 2em;
}
```

In this example, the 1.5em that's defined on the .box element will be equal to 30px—remember, a single em is equal to whatever the font size is set to, making it 20px plus half of 20px. But on the child paragraph element (<p>), the value of em will be 28px. This is because the font size is set on that element at 14px, making the padding equal to 14px doubled.

Following so far? If you're still confused, Table 3.1 may help you grasp how ems are related to font size.

Table 3.1. Ems related to font size in pixels

	14px	15px	16px	17px	18px
1em	14px	15px	16px	17px	18px
1.5em	21px	22.5px	24px	25.5px	27px
2em	28px	30px	32px	34px	36px
2.5em	35px	37.5px	40px	42.5px	45px
3em	42px	45px	48px	51px	54px

The top row represents the font size for any given element. The left column represents the em units. So, for example, if the font size is 15px and you declare 2.5em for something on that element, just run your finger across until you find the cell that intersects 2.5em and 15px. This brings you to the cell that says 37.5px (or, 15px multiplied by 2.5).

Rem Units

This is a newer CSS unit that's worth getting to know. As you can see from the em unit example we just discussed, em units can be a bit tricky to deal with, especially when their value is inherited from a parent element. The rem unit seeks to solve this problem by calculating its value based on the font size of the `<html>` element.

Let's use the same HTML from the em unit example to demonstrate rem units:

```css
html {
    font-size: 22px;
}

.box {
    font-size: 20px;
    padding: 1.5em;
}

p {
    font-size: 14px;
    padding: 2rem;
}
```

Notice we've defined rem units on the paragraph element's padding, but we've kept the em unit on the padding of the `.box` element. So what will the "2rem" value compute to?

Instead of calculating their value based on the element's `font-size` value, rem units calculate their value based on the `font-size` value set on the root element (hence "rem," or "root em"). In all HTML pages, the root element is the `<html>` element. So whatever font size is defined on that element (or whatever value the browser assigns to it by default), will be equal to a single rem unit.

To understand this a little better, refer back to Table 3.1 from the previous section on em units. All the values in the chart remain the same. In the case of em units, the top row of pixel values represents the font-size value for the element on which the ems are applied. But when using rem units, the top row of pixel values would represent the font-size value for the `<html>` element of the page on which the rems are applied.

The last point to mention here is that browser support for rem units is very good, but not perfect. Older versions of Internet Explorer (versions 6-8) do not support rem units. So if you are developing a website that has a large number of Internet Explorer users, you may want to avoid using rems and stick with ems or pixels instead.

Percentages

A percentage unit is defined using the % character. Percentage values are always relative to another value on the element itself or on a parent element, which can sometimes make them appear confusing. For example, in the case of the .box element in the rule set shown, the 40% value will be 40% of the width of the immediate parent element:

```
.box {
    width: 40%;
}
```

So if this .box element is inside an element that is 500px wide, then the .box element's width will be equal to 200px (which is 40% of 500px). If there is no set width on the containing element, then the 40% will represent 40% of whatever the width happens to equal within the browser window. Figure 3.7 might help you understand this.

Figure 3.7. This box is set to width: 40%, making its width 40% of the available horizontal space in which it sits

The box is set to a width of 40%, and it's centered inside the available horizontal space. Notice in Figure 3.8 what happens when we increase the available space. The width is still set to 40%, but the box is wider, because the available horizontal space is larger.

This box is set to width: 40%

Figure 3.8. This box is again set at 40% width, but it's larger because the available horizontal space it sits in is larger

Integers

Some CSS properties take integers—that is, whole numbers—as values. We've already seen an example of this when we applied a z-index value to our `.logo` element:

```
.logo {
  z-index: 10;
}
```

Here we set the `z-index` property to an integer value. In the case of integers, the number is an absolute value, rather than being relative to anything else. In other words, the z-index is equal to 10, with no hidden inherited values, which is different from percentages or ems.

Keywords

We've already seen keyword values used a number of times while building RecipeFinder. For example, you might remember the code we used to center different elements on the page horizontally:

```
.center-global {
  width: 1020px;
  margin: 0 auto;
}
```

Notice the margin property uses a value of `auto`. This is an example of a keyword value. Keyword values are basically any predefined word or set of characters that form a single value for one or more properties.

One particular keyword that's available as a value for every CSS property is `inherit`. This keyword value tells the browser to inherit the value for that property from the value of the same property on its parent element.

Color Values

You've seen color values a number of times in the book so far. One of the most common types of color values is referred to as hexadecimal notation, or "hex" for short. We used this for the background color we defined on the <body> element of RecipeFinder:

```
body {
  background-color: #cab5a3;
}
```

If we desired, we could set the exact same color using another type of color value: RGB, which stands for "Red, Green, Blue." The following RGB color value will produce the exact same result as the hex color from the previous declaration:

```
body {
  background-color: rgb(202, 181, 163);
}
```

Many CSS developers find RGB color values a bit easier to work with than hex, because you can easily increment or decrement one of the three values (representing red, green, and blue) to compare colors. Incidentally, RGB values range from 0 to 255 for each of the three values inside the parentheses.

You can also use HSL color values. Let's use an online RGB to HSL converter[1] to find the HSL equivalent of the RGB color we defined in the previous example. Here's the HSL notation:

```
body {
  background-color: hsl(28, 27%, 72%);
}
```

HSL stands for Hue, Saturation, and Lightness, which are what the three values inside the parentheses represent. The first value (the hue,) takes a value from 0 to

---

[1] http://serennu.com/colour/hsltorgb.php

359, with each number representing a different hue, or shade. The second value represents the saturation level of the chosen hue—that is, how strong the hue should appear—and is defined using a percentage. Finally, the lightness value tells the browser how much white, or lightness, to add to the hue. A level of 50% is "normal," while 100% lightness will make any chosen color white, and 0% lightness will make any color black.

In other words, each of the following examples will produce a background color of pure white, even though they have different hue and saturation values:

```
body {
  background-color: hsl(28, 37%, 100%);
}

p {
  background-color: hsl(156, 40%, 100%);
}
```

And the following two examples will both produce pure black, even though, again, the hue and saturation levels are different:

```
body {
  background-color: hsl(245, 63%, 0%);
}

p {
  background-color: hsl(59, 20%, 0%);
}
```

Transparency

There are a few different ways to achieve partially transparent or semi-opaque elements on a web page. The best-known way to do this is by means of images; that is, using either a transparent GIF image or a transparent PNG image. You can use Photoshop or virtually any other image editor to create semi-transparent images.

To avoid having to create extra image files, you can achieve transparency on an HTML page using one of three different CSS features.

The Opacity Property

The opacity property lets you define how opaque an element should be. Let's use the opacity property on our logo, if only temporarily:

```
.logo {
  opacity: .5;
}
```

The opacity property takes a number value from 0 to 1, so you're allowed to use decimal values. Our example sets the opacity to `.5`. If we add this declaration to the existing styles on our `.logo` element, it'll cause the logo to appear 50% opaque (or, you could say, 50% transparent). Figure 3.9 displays a comparison of the logo before and after adding the opacity property at 50% transparency.

Figure 3.9. The RecipeFinder logo with and without CSS transparency using the opacity property

Internet Explorer versions prior to version 9 don't support the opacity property, but you can mimic the same effect using a special filter that works only in those older versions of IE. So, if you wanted full browser support for the opacity property, you would have to do this:

```
.logo {
  -ms-filter: "progid:DXImageTransform.Microsoft.Alpha(opacity=50)";
  filter: alpha(opacity=50);
  opacity: .5;
}
```

Don't worry about the syntax of those first two lines; you can copy and paste those from a number of sources online.[2] The only parts of the code that you need to change

---

[2] For example, http://www.impressivewebs.com/css-opacity-reference/.

are the values. On the first two lines, the 50 value represents 50 out of 100, which is equivalent to the .5 value for the opacity property. In other words, if the opacity property was set to a value of .34, the code with equivalent, old-IE syntax would look like this:

```
.logo {
  -ms-filter: "progid:DXImageTransform.Microsoft.Alpha(opacity=34)";
  filter: alpha(opacity=34);
  opacity: .34;
}
```

Fortunately, because fewer and fewer people are using older versions of Internet Explorer, you're unlikely to need to do this very often, if ever. Also, opacity settings are a decorative feature that isn't crucial to the functioning and accessibility of a web page. So you should be okay to leave the IE filter lines out completely and allow the page to degrade to no transparency on older versions of IE. It should also be noted that those first two lines of code are not valid CSS, but they do achieve the desired result.

RGBA and HSLA Colors

The other two ways to achieve transparency levels on elements using CSS are by means of RGBA and HSLA color values. In this chapter, you've already seen the syntax for RGB and HSL color values. The "A" in RGBA and HSLA stands for "alpha," representing a transparency channel as part of the color value. Let's first use RGBA on the background color of our footer element.

In our design, the footer element has a background color with a hex value of #42031e. We haven't added that color to the footer yet, so it still looks bare. Let's set the equivalent RGB value for the footer, and add an alpha (transparency) setting to the syntax:

```
footer {
  background-color: rgba(66, 3, 30, .5);
}
```

Notice two points in this syntax, as compared to the RGB syntax we saw earlier. Firstly, the notation is rgba() instead of rgb(). Secondly, we've added a fourth comma-separated value, which represents the alpha channel. This fourth value in the parentheses is set in the same way we set opacity: Using a decimal-based number from 0 to 1.

But hold on a second! If we add this declaration to our footer element and refresh the page, you'll notice that nothing has happened (assuming you've been following the example code up to this point). The reason we don't see the background color on the footer yet is because of the float-clearing problem we talked about in Chapter 2.

Currently there are three elements inside the footer, and each of those elements has its float property set to a value of `left`. As we discussed, this means that those elements are taken out of the flow, causing their parent element to collapse, essentially ignoring them. To fix this problem, we'll add the `cf` class to our `.footer-inside` element:

```
<div class="footer-inside center-global cf">
```

Now we can see our footer's background color, and it appears as shown in Figure 3.10.

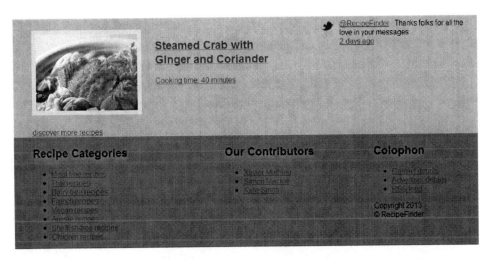

Figure 3.10. Our footer with an RGBA background color

Float Clearing 101

The float-clearing problem that sprung up again in this chapter as a result of floating the elements inside the footer could occur multiple times during a project.

So, if you're trying to figure out why a background color or background image is not appearing, the first thing you should do is add the clearfix code to that element (or `overflow: hidden`, if you prefer that method) and see if that fixes it.

What about HSLA? This works the same way as RGBA. So, if you want to define an alpha setting on any HSL color, use `hsla()` notation and add a fourth value:

```
footer {
  background-color: hsla(334, 91%, 14%, .5);
}
```

This will achieve the same result, being the equivalent color in HSL, along with the .5 alpha setting.

Having added this background color to the element, you'll notice that the shade is not exactly what we want. As we did with the `opacity` property on the `.logo` element, we'll remove the HSLA syntax, and just use plain RGB:

```
footer {
  background-color: rgb(66, 3, 30);
}
```

This gives us the background color we want, as shown in Figure 3.11.

Figure 3.11. Our footer with the correct background color

Opacity versus Color-based Transparency

If you're going to choose a method to achieve transparency on one or more elements, it's important to understand that there's a big difference between how transparency is achieved using the opacity property compared to the transparency channel of the color values we just discussed.

RGB, HSL, RGBA, and HSLA colors can be used anywhere in a CSS file where a color value is accepted (such as on backgrounds and borders). But the opacity property is applied directly on an element itself, rather than as a color value. This has one major drawback: The opacity property makes, not only, the element itself semi-transparent, but also everything inside that element. And compounding this problem is the fact that there's no way to reverse the transparency on the child elements without removing it from the parent. As you might imagine, this is often an undesirable result.

In most cases, this can be resolved by simply using a different method of achieving transparency (such as a PNG image or RGBA color), but it's good to know that this occurs, so you can decide from the outset which transparency method is ideal. For example, the opacity property would be best used on an image inserted via the <img> tag whereas RGBA or HSLA transparency would be more suited for a solid background color or transparency applied to text.

Other Values

There are additional types of values you might come across, or find useful, (for example, ex, pt, or deg). We don't have the space to go into all of them in detail here. Some will be covered to a degree in later chapters, but for the most part, the values we've discussed in this chapter are those you'll use most often.

Other values are useful in certain circumstances too, so try to become familiar with some of those as well. If you're up for it, you can find a full list and explanation of each value in the official specification.[3]

---

[3] http://www.w3.org/TR/css3-values/

Adding Shadows to Elements

The RecipeFinder website is starting to show a little bit of color and style, but Figure 3.12 reveals what else is missing from our design.

Figure 3.12. Our original design has shadows that we haven't yet added

Notice the red arrows pointing at various elements in Figure 3.12. All of these have something in common: a subtle shadow attached to them, adding some depth to the design.

We could achieve that look using images, but it's messy to do, sometimes requiring extra HTML elements, or some kind of JavaScript trick. We can do it with pure CSS, and the shadows we add will be flexible and easy to change should we want to make any adjustments to them in the future.

Adding a Shadow to the Header

First, let's add a shadow to the <header> element—the one at the top of the website that sits above the big promo image. For this, we're going to use the box-shadow property:

```
body > header {
  box-shadow: rgba(0, 0, 0, .25) 0 3px 2px 0;
  position: relative;
  z-index: 10;
}
```

Before I explain what we've done with the box-shadow property, notice that we've also positioned the <header> element relatively and added a z-index value of 10. This is the same z-index setting we added to the .logo element.

After adding the box shadow without the z-index setting, you'll see that the shadow doesn't overlay the image. This is because the big promo image appears after the <header> in our HTML, thus overlapping it. Adding the new z-index declaration fixes this problem. Also, since the .logo element is actually a child of the <header>, we can remove the z-index declaration from that rule set, since all elements inside the <header> will have the same z-index value as the <header> itself.

This is the kind of situation that happens often during a project: you'll add one or more CSS properties to an element and those new properties will make other existing properties redundant, or ineffective. So try to keep a mental note of the properties you're adding throughout your project, and remove any redundant code.

The box-shadow property accepts up to six values. Here are those values in detail:

▨ a color value (RGB, HSLA, hex, etc), which defines the color of the shadow

▨ a horizontal offset (set with a length value)

▨ a vertical offset (length)

▨ Blur (a length value defining how blurry the shadow should appear)

▨ Spread (length defining how far the shadow should spread)

▨ An optional inset keyword is also allowed, which tells the browser to place the shadow on the inside of the element, rather than outside it.

▨ Multiple shadows can be added to a single element by comma separated sets of values.

In this case, our box shadow has no horizontal offset and no blur, and does not use the inset keyword. Also, the color we're using is pure black (represented by three zeros in RGB,) and we've added an alpha value, setting the transparency level of the black to 75% transparent (or 25% opaque). After adding these new styles, our <header> should look like Figure 3.13.

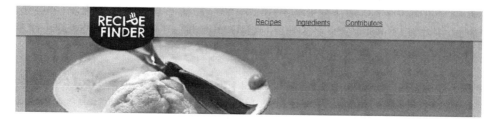

Figure 3.13. A box shadow added to the bottom of the header

We're still missing the background on the <header>, which is actually a gradient—that is, a combination of colors, transitioned smoothly. We'll be discussing gradients later in the book, so we'll leave this as-is for now.

Adding a Shadow below the Promo Image

What else requires a drop shadow? Below the promo image, we have something a little tricky. There's not only the drop shadow, but just above that there's a thick border, which is attached to the bottom of the promo image. If we look closely at that border, we find that like the header, it's actually a gradient, as shown in Figure 3.14.

Figure 3.14. A close-up of the gradient and shadow at the bottom of the big promo section

This gradient border at the bottom of the .promo element is about 8px tall. To make room for this, we'll add 8px of padding to the bottom of the .promo element. The subject of of the gradient will be included later in the book when we cover CSS gradients. For now, we'll include the shadow, adding to the existing styles on that element:

```
.promo {
  position: relative;
  z-index: 5;
  padding-bottom: 8px;
  box-shadow: rgba(0, 0, 0, .25) 0 3px 2px 0;
}
```

This box shadow has the same values as the previous ones, keeping the look of the two shadows consistent as in our Photoshop file.

Adding Shadows to Small Images

Where else do we need to add shadows? The images in the "Latest Recipes" section also have drop shadows. Let's add a shadow to our images, changing the values for the shadow to accommodate this smaller set of elements:

```
.media img {
  float: left;
  margin-right: 30px;
  border: solid 9px #ede0d5;
  box-shadow: rgba(0, 0, 0, .25) 2px 2px 2px 0;
}
```

For this drop shadow, we've added a 2px horizontal offset (the first value after the color) and we've reduced the vertical offset by one pixel. This gives us just about the look we want; very similar to the original Photoshop mock-up.

Adding Shadows to Buttons

Finally, we have one more set of items to which we need to apply a box shadow: the two big "cook it now!" and "discover more recipes" buttons.

At this point, we haven't yet added any styles to our button elements, so they look rather plain, consisting purely of text. Later we're going to style those buttons with gradients and add the correct font, but for now, let's just add a height and width, a temporary background color as a placeholder, and the necessary box shadows:

```
.promo-btn {
  display: inline-block;
  width: 208px;
  padding: 13px 0;
  background-color: #6c0733;
  box-shadow: rgba(0, 0, 0, .25) 0 7px 2px 0;
}
```

Notice we're using the display property with a value of `inline-block`. As discussed in Chapter 2, all inline and inline-block elements are subject to text-based properties. So, this will help us to center the element later when we start styling our text.

Notice that we've also assigned a set width to the button, but not a height. Instead, we're letting the height occur as a result of top and bottom padding, defined here using padding shorthand. We've also added a background color and the necessary box shadow.

The shadow is basically the same as the others—again using black at 25% opacity—but this time the vertical offset is a little larger. Figure 3.15 shows us how the button looks at this stage.

Figure 3.15. The promo button with the shadow applied

As you can see, there's still a lot of work to do on the button, not only aesthetically, but also in terms of position on the page. Let's fix some of that right now by adding a set width to the element holding the promo text and button. You'll recall, the HTML for that section looks like this:

```
<div class="promo-desc">
<h1>Sweet and Sour Zucchini Puree</h1>
<a href="#" class="promo-btn">cook it now!</a>
</div>
```

We'll add the width to the `.promo-desc` element, like so:

```
.promo-desc {
  position: absolute;
  bottom: 93px;
  right: 75px;
  width: 316px;
}
```

Now the promo section looks like what's shown in Figure 3.16.

Figure 3.16. A width added to the `.promo-desc` element

The other button on the page appears below the "Latest Recipes" section. We're going to use many of the same styles on that button, so let's save a few lines of code by doing the following:

```
<a href="#" class="promo-btn more-btn">discover more recipes</a>
```

Here we've added the `.promo-btn` class to the **Discover more recipes** button, in addition to adding a secondary class. So this button will have all the styles of the original button, including the shadow, but then we'll make some modifications via the `.more-btn` class:

```
.more-btn {
  text-align: center;
  float: right;
```

```
    margin-right: 50px;
    width: 280px;
}
```

We'll finish up the look of those buttons in the next two chapters.

Adding the Divider Shadow

The final shadow we'll be adding to RecipeFinder is the divider that appears in between the "Latest Recipes" column and the sidebar. Figure 3.17 shows how it looks in our original design.

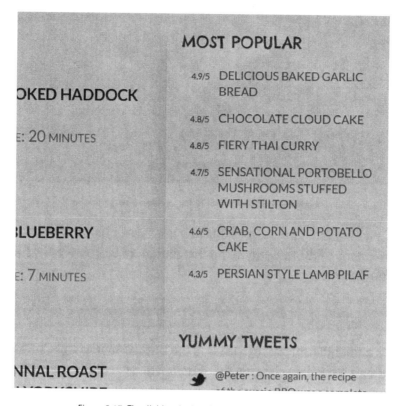

Figure 3.17. The divider shadow between the main columns

We won't be able to reproduce that shadow using just CSS, with no images. So, in this instance, we're going to revert to using an image, set as a background. After getting the image out of our Photoshop design, the image will be added to the .latest section, on the background, like this:

```
.latest {
  width: 640px;
  float: left;
  padding: 0 40px;
  background: url(../images/bg-column.png) no-repeat top right;
}
```

To position the shadow image (called **bg-column.png**), we'll use the "`top`" and "`right`" keywords, which you'll recall from our discussion on backgrounds earlier in this chapter. This positions the image at the top right of the `.latest` section, giving us the look we want.

What about text shadows?

The design for RecipeFinder doesn't incorporate any shadows on text, but if you want to apply shadows to text in your projects, you can do this easily using the text-shadow property. The syntax for `text-shadow` is very similar to `box-shadow`.

Let's add a text shadow to the "Latest Recipes" heading text so we can see how it would look. Here's the CSS:

```
h1 {
  text-shadow: rgba(0, 0, 0, .6) 5px 5px 4px;
}
```

Figure 3.18 shows us how this shadow will look on our page.

Figure 3.18. A temporary shadow added to heading text

As mentioned, this shadow is not part of the original design, so we won't be keeping it. The `text-shadow` property works exactly the same way as the `box-shadow` property, except for two key differences: There is no "spread" value allowed, and there is no option to add the `inset` keyword for `text-shadow`.

With both text shadows and box shadows, you have the ability to use any kind of color value for the color of the shadow. This is good to keep in mind, because a shadow can be used to create a number of different effects—such as an outline, or even a glow.

If you'd like to fiddle around with shadow values, there are a number of tools online that let you do this, including the CSS3 Text Shadow Generator[4] and the CSS3 Generator.[5]

 Go Easy on Shadows

As is the case with anything, you always want to be careful not to overdo it with special effects that are created in pure CSS. For example, features like shadows, gradients, and rounded corners don't use images, so some developers may feel that it's okay to add them to many elements.

Shadows in particular, however, have been demonstrated to cause web pages to slow down considerably when the user is scrolling, or when the page is loading, or even when some kind of animation is running.

Although you *can* put a shadow on every element on the page, and you also have the option to layer multiple shadows on a single element, in many cases this could be overkill and cause your page to become sluggish.

Summary

This chapter has helped us make the RecipeFinder website a little more visually enticing, adding some color and depth. Along the way, we've learned about CSS backgrounds, common units and values, different ways to achieve transparency, and how to add shadows to elements with pure CSS.

In the next chapter, we're going to cover a number of different text-related CSS features, including styling links and using custom fonts.

---

[4] http://css3gen.com/text-shadow/
[5] http://css3generator.com/

Links, Text, and Custom Fonts

Our RecipeFinder project is coming along nicely. In this chapter we have a lot of ground to cover, so let's start by taking a look at a partial screenshot of RecipeFinder (shown in Figure 4.1,) after adding all the code we've learned about in Chapters 1-3.

At this stage in the coding of our RecipeFinder website, the biggest discrepancy between the look of our page and that of the original Photoshop design is the styling of text elements. Let's learn a number of new CSS features to help us improve the text on RecipeFinder so that it looks more like the original Photoshop design.

Figure 4.1. The current state of RecipeFinder

Styling Links and Text

The first thing we're going to address here is the color of the links on the website. By default, in all web browsers, text links (that is, elements marked up using HTML's <a> tag with the href attribute,) are displayed blue and underlined.

If you recall, the original design of RecipeFinder calls for all links to have a color other than blue, and with no underline. Let's add some CSS to our stylesheet to begin correcting this:

```
a:link, a:visited {
  text-decoration: none;
}
```

You'll remember that we covered different types of CSS selectors in Chapter 1, and briefly touched on the fact that selectors can be combined using a comma. That's what we're doing in this example, and it's called **selector grouping**.

To help you understand what this accomplishes, take a look at the following code:

```
a:link {
    text-decoration: none;
}

a:visited {
    text-decoration: none;
}
```

This longhand code would produce the same result as that in the previous code block. You can easily see why the previous example is the better choice—we avoid repeating the declaration. In a large CSS file, using selector grouping can save you *hundreds* of lines of code.

Now let's discuss exactly what we're doing in that comma-separated selector group. In both of the group's selectors, we're using the element type selector to target <a> elements, and we're also using a pseudo-class for each.

The :link pseudo-class is something you'll see from time to time, but it's rarely, if ever, necessary. This pseudo-class targets all <a> elements that have an href attribute set in the HTML (i.e, they're links). Theoretically, you could have an <a> element without an href attribute defined, but you'll only occasionally see that nowadays. So, technically, we could do this instead:

```
a, a:visited {
    text-decoration: none;
}
```

Or even simply this:

```
a {
    text-decoration: none;
}
```

Notice that now we're just targeting all <a> elements directly.

The `:visited` pseudo-class targets all links on the page that have been clicked, or visited, by the user. With this pseudo-class, you can style visited links differently from other links. For RecipeFinder, we're going to keep the same styling for both visited and non-visited links, so there's no need to use a separate `:visited` rule set. But in some cases, it could improve the overall usability of a website if visited links are identified with distinct styling.

 Not Using :link

Because `:link` is somewhat redundant and adds some extra specificity, and because we won't be giving any extra styling to `:visited` links, in the stylesheet for RecipeFinder we're going to stick with targeting our links using just the element type selector, without `:link` or `:visited`, for all of our link styles.

Within the declaration block, we're using the `text-decoration` property, with a value of `none`, which removes any underline. The text-decoration property also accepts values of `underline` (the default), `overline`, and `line-through`, all of which should be self-explanatory. It's also worth noting that, although until now `text-decoration` has been treated as a single longhand property, it now represents a shorthand for multiple `text-decoration` properties, which you can read about in the official specification.[1]

Changing Link Color

Now that we've removed the underline, let's change the color of our links. We need to write more than just one declaration to do this, because different parts of the website have different colors for links.

Let's first define a global color for all text links:

```
a {
  text-decoration: none;
  color: #544a40;
}
```

And next we'll target our main navigation links at the top of the page, and our two buttons:

---

[1] http://www.w3.org/TR/css-text-decor-3/

```
nav a {
. color: #fefefe;
}
```

As you can see, this example uses the descendant combinator to target the links. You may recall from Chapter 1 that this is done by means of a space between two selectors—in this case targeting all <a> tags that are inside of the <nav> element.

These last two rule sets use the color property to change the text color of the links. Thus far in the book, we've used the color property in a few examples. In most cases, you'll use it to set the text color of an element, but the color property actually represents more than just text color.

The color property defines all foreground colors on that element, and this includes borders, list bullets, and even the text that appears in place of an image when an image doesn't load—defined in the HTML using the alt attribute on an <img> tag.

 Targeting multiple <nav>, <header>, or <footer> tags

In this book, we're adding styles to a phony website called RecipeFinder, which consists of just a single web page. In our HTML for this web page, we're using one <nav> element, one <header> element, and one <footer> element.

HTML5, however, allows us to define multiple <nav>, <header>, or <footer> elements on a single page. Thus, if we were to add more of these elements to the page, all the styles that we applied to those elements would also apply to the new elements. This might not be the desired result.

To target multiple <nav>, <header>, or <footer> tags uniquely, we would have to use a different selector, or use selector grouping. You can also add class names and use the class selector, or some other type of selector, depending on the context of the elements.

Another area on the page that needs a change in link styles is the "Yummy Tweets" section in the sidebar. Let's fix those and then move on to something else before we take care of the rest of the link styles on the page:

```
.tweet a {
  color: #810430;
}
```

```
.tweet .date {
  color: #8f7e6d;
}
```

We've made two changes here: set the color for all links inside an individual tweet; and set a unique color for the link that's at the bottom of each tweet, which tells the user when the tweet was sent. You'll recall from Chapter 2 that each tweet's date is wrapped in a <div> element that has a class of "date", so we've used that class in our CSS to apply the unique styles.

 Setting Global Styles

The styles we added to all links on the page are what we might term "global" styles, because they apply to all links on the page that aren't styled otherwise. These differ from styles applied to links that are in a certain context (such as links in a .tweet element). There are other global styles that you'll want to get in the habit of adding to your CSS at the start of a project.

One such example is the text color set on the <body> element. The RecipeFinder design doesn't have any common text elements—like a paragraph of text—that we can use to identify a global text color. But we can use something like a dark gray that's commonly used for body text:

```
body {
  background: #cab5a3 url(../images/bg-main.gif) repeat
➥repeat 0 0;
  color: #333;
}
```

In our case, this won't be particularly noticeable after we finish styling the rest of the text on the page. That said, it'll serve as a default text color everywhere that text color isn't specifically defined.

Similarly, you might have other generic font styles applied to elements like h1, h2, h3, p, and so forth. Although we're not doing this extensively on RecipeFinder, it's something you'll want to do on most projects. This'll help you avoid having to add too many unnecessary classes on elements that can just be styled by targeting them using the element type selector.

Later in this chapter, we'll fix up the rest of the text styles for all the sections of RecipeFinder, but for now let's discover the concept of embedding custom web fonts, which you'll be doing often on the websites you build.

Using Custom Web Fonts

At this point, there are a few style changes we want to make to the text on RecipeFinder, including changing the size of the text. But before we attempt that, we need to get the correct fonts to display on our web page. For this design, we've used two custom fonts, shown in Figure 4.2—a screenshot depicting part of the sidebar in the original Photoshop design.

Figure 4.2. RecipeFinder uses two different fonts, both used in the Most Popular section in the sidebar

The heading that says "Most Popular" is set using a font called "Chelsea Market" and the other text is set using a font called "Lato." You'll notice these are the two primary fonts used in our design. Let's define them in our CSS and see what happens.

Of the two fonts, Lato is the most prevalent throughout the page, with Chelsea Market being used mainly for headings. Here's what we'll do:

```
body {
  background: #cab5a3 url(../images/bg-main.gif) repeat repeat 0 0;
  color: #333;
  font-family: Lato;
}
```

You'll see we've added a declaration to the rule set defining the styles for the `<body>` element on RecipeFinder. This new declaration defines the `font-family` property, with the Lato font as the property's value. `font-family` accepts one or more font names, separated by commas. So in this case, we could expand the declaration to look like this:

```
body {
  background: #cab5a3 url(../images/bg-main.gif) repeat repeat 0 0;
  color: #333;
  font-family: Lato, Arial, Helvetica, sans-serif;
}
```

But if we apply this declaration to our website and refresh the page, we won't see anything change. This is because, in order to display a font on a web page using the `font-family` property, the user who visits the web page needs to have that font installed on their computer or mobile device's operating system. Most users are probably not going to have the Lato font installed, which is why we're not seeing it displayed. In this situation, we're seeing the default sans-serif font, which is specified in **Normalize.css** (which we added to RecipeFinder in Chapter 2). Without **Normalize.css**, you would likely see a serif font like Times New Roman.

 Commonly Installed Fonts

> If you would like to know the fonts that are commonly installed on most computers, see http://www.ampsoft.net/webdesign-l/WindowsMacFonts.html.

When separating the font names via commas in the font-family declaration, we're defining what's called a **font stack**. The browser will read this and then display the first font that it recognizes. Just in case none of the fonts are defined, the last option we've included is a generic font family. This tells the browser to display the text using the default sans-serif font that's installed on the user's system. Other generic font families include serif, monospace, and cursive. We've chosen sans-serif because the Lato font is a sans-serif font—that is, it doesn't have serifs, which are small lines that trail from the extremities of the font[2].

Using @font-face

While it 's good to know how to stack fonts to ensure there's a back-up plan for when the original font isn't available, we want to do whatever we can to make sure the primary font is loaded. To do this, we have to include the font using `@font-face`. You'll recall, in Chapter 2, we briefly learned about the `@media` at-rule. `@font-face` is another type of at-rule. It enables us to embed custom fonts in our stylesheet and then use them by name, employing the `font-family` property.

Here's how we set the `@font-face` rule to include the Lato font on RecipeFinder:

```
@font-face {
    font-family: Lato;
    src: url('lato-regular-webfont.eot');
    src: url('lato-regular-webfont.eot?#iefix') format
➡('embedded-opentype'),
         url('lato-regular-webfont.woff') format('woff'),
         url('lato-regular-webfont.ttf') format('truetype'),
         url('lato-regular-webfont.svg#latoregular') format('svg');
    font-weight: normal;
    font-style: normal;
}
```

Rest assured that this section of code is not as complicated as it looks. In the majority of situations where it'll be employed, it won't be necessary to understand much about it.

What this section does is include the Lato font, using all of the code necessary to ensure it loads on as many browsers and operating systems as possible. The only parts of this code that it's useful to be familiar with are: the file names of the different font files, which should all point to valid files (more on this in a moment); and the font-family declaration at the top, which is the name of the font we'll use later in the CSS (and which we've already used in one declaration block example in this chapter).

---

[2] http://en.wikipedia.org/wiki/Sans-serif

To ensure cross-browser compatibility, the syntax for the `@font-face` at-rule embeds the font using four different font types (EOT, WOFF, TTF, and SVG). The browser will load whichever version of the font it can. And it does this without loading any of the other versions, thus giving the user the fastest (and therefore best,) possible experience.

There's much more to this syntax than we have the space to cover here. To read up on this subject, check out the article "The New Bulletproof @font-face Syntax" on fontspring.com.[3]

Including the Different Font Files

If we examine the big `@font-face` code block above, we see that it references four different font files that we haven't yet included in our project's source files. So how do we do we go about adding these?

For the RecipeFinder website, we intentionally selected a pair of fonts that are freely available for embedding as web fonts. That's to ensure we don't have to worry about font licensing issues. Whenever including a font using `@font-face`, it's important that the font specifically allows for embedding using `@font-face`. Some fonts can be included on web pages using images or another format, but not via `@font-face`—even if it's been paid for. So be sure to check the font license before making your choice.

The safest way to find free fonts that allow `@font-face` embedding is to use an online font service that specializes in free web fonts. Two highly recommended services are Google Web Fonts[4] and FontSquirrel.[5] Both the Lato and Chelsea Market fonts are available on Google Web Fonts, so that's the service we've used to obtain these free fonts.

When choosing a font using Google Web Fonts, it's not required to download the font and include it in the website's source files. Instead, simply use Google's linked CSS file for that particular font, and Google will do the heavy lifting. Figure 4.3 shows the code for the Lato font as it appears on Google Web Fonts, ready to copy and paste.

---

[3] http://www.fontspring.com/blog/the-new-bulletproof-font-face-syntax
[4] http://www.google.com/fonts/
[5] http://www.fontsquirrel.com/

Figure 4.3. The code for the `<link>` tag to include a font from Google Web Fonts

You can find this code for any font on the Google Web Fonts service by searching for the font, then clicking the **Quick Use** button for that font.

If we decided to use this method to include Lato, this chunk of code would be placed in our HTML, above our other CSS file references, like this:

```
<link href='http://fonts.googleapis.com/css?family=Lato:400,700'
➥ rel='stylesheet' type='text/css'>
<link rel="stylesheet" href="css/normalize.css">
<link rel="stylesheet" href="css/styles.css">
```

This uses the `<link>` tag that we learned about in Chapter 1, where we discussed all the different ways to include CSS in a web page. Once we have that in place, we just need to define the font-family property in our CSS using the correct name for the font. We can see the name referenced in the URL, where it says "`family=Lato`". So, in this instance, our font declared for the `<body>` element would look like this, with fallbacks listed:

```
body {
  background: #cab5a3 url(../images/bg-main.gif) repeat repeat 0 0;
  color: #333;
  font-family: Lato, Arial, Helvetica, sans-serif;
}
```

RecipeFinder includes the Lato font in two different styles: regular and bold. These styles are represented by the numbers "400" (for regular) and "700" (for bold), and these are appended to the file reference in the `<link>` tag so that Google knows which font variations to reference in the CSS file. And so, if we want to include the Lato font in bold, we do the following:

```
body {
  background: #cab5a3 url(../images/bg-main.gif) repeat repeat 0 0;
  color: #333;
  font-family: Lato, Arial, Helvetica, sans-serif;
  font-weight: 700;
}
```

This declaration block uses another new property, the `font-weight` property. This defines the weight, or heaviness, of the font. The default is "normal", and it can also be set to "bold", "lighter", "bolder", or the numbers "100", "200", "300", up to "900"—but only in increments of 100. It's worth noting, however, that these different values will work only if the font itself allows for the weights specified.

In this example, we could use either a value of "700" or a value of "bold"—they have exactly the same effect as one another.

Generating the Font Files

In the case of RecipeFinder, we're not going to use the Google Web Font embedded `<link>` tag code. Instead, we'll use the @font-face declaration directly. We're taking this slightly more complicated route so that we can cover the full process of adding a licensed custom font to a web page. As mentioned earlier, the typical cross-browser syntax for `@font-face` includes four different files. Let's find the Lato and Chelsea Market fonts on Google Web Fonts so we can generate all the files we'll need.

Go to Google Web Fonts and type "Chelsea" in the search field on the left side of the page, as shown in Figure 4.4

Figure 4.4. Finding the Chelsea Market font on Google Web Fonts

You'll see the Chelsea Market font appear on the right side in the search results. Click the button that says **Add to Collection**, as shown in Figure 4.5.

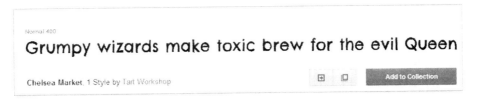

Figure 4.5. Each font on Google Web Fonts has an **Add to Collection** option

This adds the font to a temporary collection that we can download at any time. Now do the same for the Lato font: search for it, and then add it to your collection.

After adding these two fonts, you should see a message at the bottom of the screen that says "2 font families in your Collection". You should also see a link at the top right portion of the window that says "Download your Collection". Click the download button, and you'll see the message shown in Figure 4.6.

Figure 4.6. A warning about downloading the fonts

Ignore the warning next to the red exclamation mark. That's just a reminder that you don't have to actually download the fonts, since Google hosts them for you, and lets you embed them with the `<link>` tag, as shown in the previous section. However, on this occasion, we're going to do this manually purely to learn the process. So ignore the warning and continue to download the file by clicking the link **Download the font families in your Collection as a zip-file.**

When prompted, choose a location on your computer to save the zip file, then find the file and unzip it. Once unzipped, there'll be two different folders: one for Chelsea Market, and the other for Lato. In the Chelsea Market folder there's only a single TTF font file, so let's start with that.

We want to take that file and use it to produce three additional font files, and we can do so using another free service, this one provided by FontSquirrel. It's called the Webfont Generator,[6] and it's very easy to use.

Go to the Webfont Generator URL and click the button that says **Add Fonts.**

When we click that button, we'll be prompted with a system file dialog, asking us to add a font. Navigate to the font collection we downloaded from Google Web Fonts, find the TTF font for Chelsea Market, and select it to be uploaded.

Now we'll repeat the process for the Lato font, again clicking the **Add Fonts** button and then navigating to the Lato folder. This time, there'll be ten different TTF font

---

[6] http://www.fontsquirrel.com/tools/webfont-generator

files. We don't need them all, so select only the ones called **Lato-Regular.ttf** and **Lato-Bold.ttf**. Once all three files are added, the Webfont Generator page should look as shown in Figure 4.7.

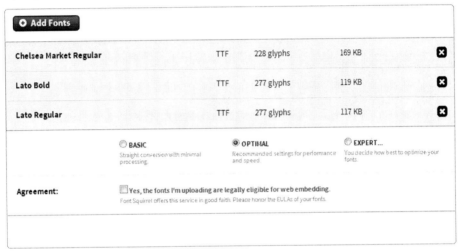

Figure 4.7. After adding three fonts to the Webfont Generator

Notice the red text next to the checkbox that says, "Yes, the fonts I'm uploading are legally eligible for web embedding." Since we know that these fonts are legally eligible for embedding, we'll go ahead and check that box. A **Download Your Kit** button will now appear. Click it to download all the files necessary for embedding the Chelsea Market and Lato fonts.

Once the zip file that FontSquirrel generates has downloaded, open it to find all the files we need, including a sample CSS and HTML file to show us how to include the fonts in our CSS. Open the file called "**stylesheet.css**" in a text editor to see three different @font-face declarations. Copy all three of those and put them into the RecipeFinder CSS file, just before the declaration block that targets the <body> tag. Our CSS should look something like this:

```
@font-face {
    font-family: 'chelsea_marketregular';
    src: url('chelseamarket-regular-webfont.eot');
    src: url('chelseamarket-regular-webfont.eot?#iefix') format
➥('embedded-opentype'),
        url('chelseamarket-regular-webfont.woff') format('woff'),
        url('chelseamarket-regular-webfont.ttf') format('truetype'),
        url('chelseamarket-regular-webfont.svg#chelsea
➥_marketregular') format('svg');
    font-weight: normal;
    font-style: normal;
}

@font-face {
    font-family: 'latobold';
    src: url('lato-bold-webfont.eot');
    src: url('lato-bold-webfont.eot?#iefix') format('embedded-
➥opentype'),
        url('lato-bold-webfont.woff') format('woff'),
        url('lato-bold-webfont.ttf') format('truetype'),
        url('lato-bold-webfont.svg#latobold') format('svg');
    font-weight: normal;
    font-style: normal;
}

@font-face {
  font-family: 'latoregular';
  src: url('lato-regular-webfont.eot');
  src: url('lato-regular-webfont.eot?#iefix') format('embedded-
➥opentype'),
        url('lato-regular-webfont.woff') format('woff'),
        url('lato-regular-webfont.ttf') format('truetype'),
        url('lato-regular-webfont.svg#latoregular') format('svg');
  font-weight: normal;
  font-style: normal;
}

body {
  background: #cab5a3 url(../images/bg-main.gif) repeat repeat 0 0;
  color: #333;
  font-family: Lato, Arial, Helvetica, sans-serif;
}
```

Now we have all three fonts referenced in our CSS, but we have to make sure the
file references are correct. Let's go back to the zip file of generated fonts we down-

loaded from FontSquirrel, so we can grab the 12 files we need for this: the EOT, WOFF, TTF, and SVG versions of each of the three fonts.

Let's create a folder in our website's main folder called **fonts**, and copy all 12 of those files into that new fonts folder. Assuming our CSS file is inside a folder of its own, the font file references in our `@font-face` declarations are now incorrect. So, our next job is to make some changes to our `@font-face` declarations. Here's the one for Chelsea Market, corrected:

```
@font-face {
    font-family: 'ChelseaMarket';
    src: url('../fonts/chelseamarket-regular-webfont.eot');
    src: url('../fonts/chelseamarket-regular-webfont.eot?#iefix')
➡ format('embedded-opentype'),
        url('../fonts/chelseamarket-regular-webfont.woff') format
➡('woff'),
        url('../fonts/chelseamarket-regular-webfont.ttf') format
➡('truetype'),
        url('../fonts/chelseamarket-regular-webfont.svg#chelsea_
➡marketregular') format('svg');
    font-weight: normal;
    font-style: normal;
}
```

Notice that a few things have been changed here. `../fonts/` has been added in front of all the file references, which matches the fact that the files are located up one level in relation to the CSS file, and inside the **fonts** folder.

The other change to note is the value for `font-family` to `ChelseaMarket`. The previous value (`chelsea_marketregular`) would work fine, but was tricky to remember. This name, as defined in this location, can be anything we want. We just have to ensure that we use the exact same name when we reference this font in our CSS, which we'll do in a moment.

With that in place, we can make similar changes to our two Lato `@font-face` declarations:

```
@font-face {
    font-family: 'LatoBold';
    src: url('../fonts/lato-bold-webfont.eot');
    src: url('../fonts/lato-bold-webfont.eot?#iefix') format('
```

```
➥embedded-opentype'),
        url('../fonts/lato-bold-webfont.woff') format('woff'),
        url('../fonts/lato-bold-webfont.ttf') format('truetype'),
        url('../fonts/lato-bold-webfont.svg#latobold') format
➥('svg');
    font-weight: normal;
    font-style: normal;
}

@font-face {
    font-family: 'Lato';
    src: url('../fonts/lato-regular-webfont.eot');
    src: url('../fonts/lato-regular-webfont.eot?#iefix') format('
➥embedded-opentype'),
        url('../fonts/lato-regular-webfont.woff') format('woff'),
        url('../fonts/lato-regular-webfont.ttf') format('truetype'),
        url('../fonts/lato-regular-webfont.svg#latoregular') format
➥('svg');
    font-weight: normal;
    font-style: normal;
```

With those three declarations ready and using the correct file references, we can reference any of those fonts on any element on the page, and the browser will render the font in harmony with the original design.

@font-face Review

So far in this chapter, we've covered a lot of ground in regards to @font-face and embedding web fonts. Just to help you grasp all this info, here are the main points to take away:

- Custom web fonts can be included on a web page using any number of web font services, including free services such as Google Web Fonts and FontSquirrel.

- If you don't use @font-face, you may only use fonts that are available on a user's operating system.

- The most effective way to ensure cross-browser support for your custom embedded fonts is to use the @font-face syntax that references four different font files.

- After embedding any custom font using `@font-face`, you need to use the font-family property in your declaration blocks to specify where that font should be used on the page.

- The name of the font defined in the `font-family` property needs to be the exact same `font-family` name defined in the `@font-face` declaration.

- To ensure the best experience possible, you can define a font stack on the `font-family` property, for those rare instances when the custom font doesn't load.

- To use a font with `@font-face`, you must read the license for that font and ensure that it allows for `@font-face` embedding. This is necessary even if you have paid for the font.

Using Our New Fonts on RecipeFinder

As we've seen from this chapter so far, web fonts are a complex matter to deal with. Now that we have our fonts embedded on our page, and ready to use, let's see where we can identify some further uses for them. We'll also make some other typographical adjustments and, in the process, cover a few new CSS properties.

So far, we've applied the Lato Regular font (the non-bold version of Lato) on our `<body>` element. Fonts defined using `font-family` are inherited by child elements, so this applies the Lato font to all the text on the page. Not all CSS properties behave like this—something you'll learn from gaining more experience with different CSS properties. For example, applying 20px of padding to the `<body>` element would apply the padding only to the `<body>`, not to any elements inside the `<body>`.

In our original design, the main navigation and all the headings use Chelsea Market—one of the other fonts we embedded with `@font-face`. Not only that, but all the text set in Chelsea Market is in uppercase. Here's the CSS we're going to add to our stylesheet:

```
h1, h2, nav {
    font-family: ChelseaMarket, Arial, Helvetica, sans-serif;
    text-transform: uppercase;
    font-weight: normal;
}
```

The first thing to note is that we're grouping selectors so we can target multiple element types at once. It's also worth noting that, although we've applied the Chelsea Market font to all of our `<h2>` elements, we'll have to override that behaviour later in our CSS file for some of our other `<h2>` elements, which don't use Chelsea Market.

Next, after we set the Chelsea Market font, with fallbacks in the font stack, we've also added a new CSS property, the `text-transform` property. In addition to `uppercase` (which sets all the text to uppercase for those elements), this property can accept values of `capitalize` (which makes the first letter of every word uppercase), `lowercase`, and `none` (which is the default). Lastly, we've set the `font-weight` for these elements to `normal`. By default, all browsers add certain levels of styling for heading elements (`<h1>`, `<h2>`, `<h3>`, etc.), including bold, and we want to ensure that the Chelsea Market font displays without any browser-added styles.

After adding that rule set, our page should look something like Figure 4.8.

Figure 4.8. After adding our custom fonts and making the Chelsea Market text uppercase

Before we move on to the Lato font and the headings further down on the page, let's address the size and alignment of the text in the main navigation. We already added the uppercasing, but what else is missing? There are two things we can correct here: First, we'll bump the size of the font up to 20px, and then we'll fix an extra margin issue.

In our CSS, we already have a selector targeting the list items inside our navigation, so let's add one line to that rule set, and add another rule set below it:

```
nav ul li {
  display: inline-block;
  *display: inline; /* for IE7 */
  margin-right: 30px;
  font-size: 20px;
```

```
}

nav ul li:last-child {
  margin-right: 0;
}
```

Here we've adjusted the font size to 20px, which adds to the existing styles on our list items inside the `<nav>` element. But more importantly, we've introduced a new selector: the `:last-child` pseudo-class.

In Chapter 2, we added a 30px right margin on all of our list items. This caused the navigation section to be pushed too far to the left. We also set the `<nav>` section to have 177px of right margin, but there's an extra 30px added to that because of the 30px right margin set on the last list item.

The `:last-child` pseudo-class used in combination with the "nav ul li" selector tells the browser to target only the last list item. Here we've set the right margin back to 0, giving us the correct amount of space.

This is a good method to keep in mind because it's often desirable to remove styles on specific elements—say, the first or last element. CSS offers not only `:last-child`, but also `:first-child`, and a number of other pseudo-classes.[7] Using these specialized selectors prevents us from having to add extra classes or IDs to elements, which would be the only other way, using CSS, that we could target a single list item in an HTML list that has more than one list item.

Cleaning Things Up

Now that we've corrected the look of the text in the navigation, let's see what else we can improve. The text in the promo area that overlays the big promo photo needs to be aligned differently, so let's fix that by adding to the existing styles in our `.promo-desc` declaration block:

```
.promo-desc {
  position: absolute;
  bottom: 93px;
  right: 75px;
```

---

[7] http://reference.sitepoint.com/css/css3psuedoclasses

```
    width: 316px;
    text-align: center;
}
```

Here we've added the `text-align` property with a value of `center`. This property can take a value of `left`, `right`, `center`, or `justify`. Using `center` here, not only is the text centered, but this also centers the button that appears below the text. As we learned earlier in the book, the button (which is an `<a>` element in the HTML) is an inline element converted to an inline-block element, thus it's subject to typographic styles. If this were a block-level element such as `<div>` or `<p>`, and were not converted to inline-block, it would not center, because block-level elements are not in text flow and, as a result, are not subject to typographic styles.

We would also like to set the correct color for the various headings on the page. Most of these have the same color, so what we'll do is expand on the grouped selector rule set we defined a little earlier:

```
h1, h2, nav {
    font-family: ChelseaMarket, Arial, Helvetica, sans-serif;
    text-transform: uppercase;
    font-weight: normal;
    color: #810430;
}
```

Here we've added the color property set to a value of #810430, which is a burgundy shade that is sampled from the original Photoshop file. Two of our headings, however, shouldn't be this color—they should be a near-white shade. These headings have been indicated in Figure 4.9.

Figure 4.9. Some of our headings are the wrong color

Let's correct the colors on those two headings now, matching what's in our design and overriding the burgundy we just set:

```
.promo-desc h1 {
  color: #fefefe;
}
```

Once again, we're using the descendant combinator that we learned about in Chapter 1 to target the <h1> element inside the .promo-desc element.

Next we'll correct the look of the <h2> headings that appear inside the .media blocks that we defined in our CSS earlier in the book. Here's the code, targeting all <h2> elements inside .media blocks:

```
.media h2 {
  color: #49301a;
  font-family: LatoBold, Arial, Helvetica, sans-serif;
  font-weight: normal;
```

```
    font-size: 26px;
    margin-bottom: 5px;
}
```

There's something that might seem a bit paradoxical here. After defining the font as `LatoBold` (along with the fallback fonts), the next declaration defines the `font-weight` property as `normal` (as opposed to `bold`), which removes bolding from the font. So why would we remove the bolding from a font that's naturally bold?

Well, the font itself has a certain level of bolding already built in. That's why it's called Lato Bold. As we've already noted, heading elements are set as bold by browsers, as a default. This default setting makes the font bolder than we want, so, in this case, we're better off removing it. In addition to this, we've defined the correct font size for these headings.

Next we'll fix the styles for the text that appears under each of the `<h2>` headings inside the `.media` elements. This text appears inside paragraph tags. And while we're at it, we'll correct the margin spacing between the `<h2>` and the paragraph so it's more in line with the original design:

```
.media p {
  margin: 0;
  font-family: Lato, Arial, Helvetica, sans-serif;
  font-size: 18px;
  color: #7b6047;
  text-transform: uppercase;
}

.media p span {
  font-size: 25px;
}
```

There aren't any new properties here, but we have added a new rule set, targeting `<span>` elements inside paragraphs in the `.media` blocks. Why did we include this? Figure 4.10 shows us how the original design looks for each `.media` element in the "Latest Recipes" section.

Figure 4.10. A single "Latest Recipes" entry from our original design

Notice that the number indicating the minutes for cooking time is bigger than the rest of the text. With CSS, there's no way to target a specific section of a piece of text that is in the middle of a block of text, so here's what we've done in our HTML:

```
<div class="media">
    <a href="#">
        <img src="images/haddock.jpg" alt="Haddock skewers">
        <h2>Zesty Smoked Haddock Skewers</h2>
        <p>Cooking time: <span>20</span> minutes</p>
    </a>
</div>
```

Notice the <span> tags wrapped around the number. By doing this, we now can style that part of the text in any way we want. In this case, increasing the font size does the trick.

We also want to give the text for our two button elements the correct size and color, so let's do that now:

```
.promo-btn {
  display: inline-block;
  width: 208px;
  padding: 13px 0;
  background-color: #6c0733;
  box-shadow: rgba(0, 0, 0, .25) 0 7px 2px 0;
  font-size: 20px;
  color: #fefefe;
}
```

Remember that the `.promo-btn` class applies to both buttons, working as a base rule set. The second button also has a class of `.more-btn`, which allows us to add other styles that are unique to the second button.

Styling the Footer Section

We have a few other formatting improvements we want to make to our page, in particular in the footer and the sidebar. You'll recall that in Chapter 2, we took care of the layout of both the footer and the section in the sidebar called "Most Popular," and we started to fix the styles in the "Yummy Tweets" section earlier in this chapter. We'll now clean up the look of the text in those sections.

Let's run through the additions to the different parts of the footer. First, we want to remove all the list bullets from the unordered lists in all the footer sections, and fix some of the margins and padding to match the design. We'll do this by adding to an existing declaration block, and adding a new declaration block to target the `<ul>` elements in the footer:

```css
footer {
  background-color: rgb(66, 3, 30);
  padding-top: 10px;
  padding-bottom: 50px;
}

...

footer ul {
  list-style: none;
  margin: 0;
  padding: 0;
}
```

Next, we'll correct the text styles for the `.footer-1` and `.footer-2` elements, which hold the sections called "Recipe Categories" and "Contributors":

```css
.footer-1 h2 {
  font-size: 36px;
}

.footer-1 ul, .footer-2 ul {
  text-align: center;
}
```

```
  font-size: 20px;
  line-height: 1.7;
}

.footer-1 li {
  float: left;
  width: 195px;
}

.footer-1 ul a,
.footer-2 ul a {
  color: #ab97a0;
}
```

Notice that, here, we're taking full advantage of grouped selectors and descendant combinators. We've also added a float to the list items in the `.footer-1` section. This helps get the two-column look that we see in the original Photoshop design.

The `line-height` Property

The chunk of code in the previous block adds a new property: `line-height`. This property defaults to a value of "`normal`" and is used to define the height of each line of text in the targeted section of the page. `line-height` is the web page equivalent to the printing industry's leading.[8]

With a little bit of experimenting, `line-height` reveals itself to be a very useful tool for optimizing the readability of text, and ensuring that it looks just the way we want it. The `line-height` property accepts values using most of the units we've discussed already, including a unitless number value, which is what we're using here, and is the recommended way to define `line-height`.

If we use a unitless number value for line-height, the value will compute to the number multiplied by the current font size of the element to which it's applied. In this case, we've defined the line-height at 1.7, with no unit. The font size for the element is set at 20 pixels. Thus, the line-height of 1.7 is equivalent to 34 pixels.

Some of the previous styles included the `.footer-2` element as part of a few grouped selectors, fixing some of the styling issues. Let's finish up our `.footer-2` section, by adding to our existing styles:

---

[8] http://en.wikipedia.org/wiki/Leading

```
.footer-2 {
  float: left;
  width: 326px;
  padding-top: 22px;
}

  .footer-2 ul {
    margin: 0 80px 0 0;
  }
```

There's nothing new here—just some alignment corrections in harmony with what's in the design.

And finally, here is the CSS for the last section in our footer, the "Colophon":

```
.footer-3 {
  float: left;
  width: 232px;
  color: #801c48;
  padding-top: 22px;
}

  .footer-3 h2, .footer-3 a {
    color: #801c48;
  }

  .footer-3 li {
    line-height: 1.7;
  }
```

Again, all familiar properties, and we've repeated the same `line-height` value on the list items.

While we're in the footer, if you've been following along with all the code step by step, you'll notice that there needs to be some space between the top of the footer and the content above it (specifically the **Discover More Recipes** button). Let's correct that now by adding a declaration to our `.main` rule set:

```
.main {
  padding-bottom: 33px;
}
```

This rule set originally held a margin and width declaration that we later switched to a `.center-global` class in Chapter 2.

Adding Styles to Text in the Sidebar

The last change we'll make to RecipeFinder, in this chapter, is to add some styles to the text on the "Most Popular" and "Yummy Tweets" sections, found in the sidebar, in line with the original design. Let's first address the "Most Popular" section, adding to the layout styles we started to define in Chapter 2:

```css
.rating {
  float: left;
  clear: left;
  padding-top: 4px;
  padding-right: 15px;
  width: 45px;
  color: #810430;
  font-size: 13px;
}

.pop-item {
  padding-bottom: 20px;
  float: left;
  width: 250px;
  text-transform: uppercase;
  font-size: 18px;
}

.pop-item a {
  color: #544a40;
}
```

Once again we're utilizing the text-transform property, and we've defined specific font sizes. Now this section should look like Figure 4.11.

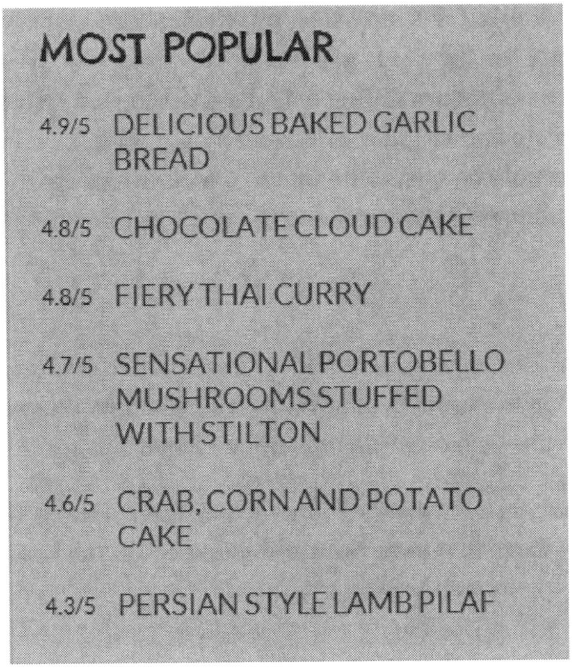

MOST POPULAR

4.9/5   DELICIOUS BAKED GARLIC
        BREAD

4.8/5   CHOCOLATE CLOUD CAKE

4.8/5   FIERY THAI CURRY

4.7/5   SENSATIONAL PORTOBELLO
        MUSHROOMS STUFFED
        WITH STILTON

4.6/5   CRAB, CORN AND POTATO
        CAKE

4.3/5   PERSIAN STYLE LAMB PILAF

Figure 4.11. The "Most Popular" section in our sidebar now has the look we want

And finally, we want to finish off the styling of the "Yummy Tweets" section. First, we'll add a line-height declaration to fix the space between lines, in harmony with the original design:

```
.tweet {
  padding-left: 55px;
  padding-right: 20px;
  position: relative;
  line-height: 1.4;
}
```

And next we'll improve the look of the text in the .date element:

```
.tweet .date {
  color: #8f7e6d;
  font-faily: Arial, sans-serif;
  color: #8f7e6d;
  font-size: 12px;
  font-style: italic;
}
```

In addition to the family, color, and size, this declaration block includes a property new to us: font-style. The font-style property does exactly what its name suggests, accepting values of normal (the default), italic, and oblique. For all intents and purposes, italic and oblique are basically the same, causing the text to slant. The difference can only be seen if the font to which this property is applied has the capability to differentiate between the two.

Summary

With all these new link and typographic styles in place, the look of RecipeFinder is very close to what we want to achieve. In fact, visually, it could pass for a pretty good-looking website—even in this incomplete form!

However, we're not quite finished. In the next chapter we're going to look at some of the fancy new effects that have been added to CSS in the last few years, and see how to add some to our web pages.

Chapter 5

Getting Fancy

The look of RecipeFinder has now advanced to the latter stages. We have the layout of all elements in place, along with all the correct fonts and text sizes.

Figure 5.1 shows a screenshot of RecipeFinder after completing all the code from Chapters 1-4.

It's looking good but, compared to our original Photoshop file, there are still a few elements missing: the background gradients on the header and button elements. As mentioned earlier, we intentionally left those unfinished so we could deal with them in this chapter, which introduces some fancy effects that you'll want to make part of your regular CSS arsenal. So let's get to it!

Figure 5.1. A screenshot showing the current state of RecipeFinder

Hover Effects

In Chapter 4, we styled the various links on RecipeFinder, adding CSS to improve their static look. However, when visiting web pages, hovering your mouse over a link or other page element will often alter its appearance. It might be a color change, a size change, or something else.

We can accomplish this in CSS by using the :hover dynamic pseudo-class. It's "dynamic" because it doesn't target an existing element; rather it targets an element in a given state (the hover state). So let's add this pseudo-class to RecipeFinder, starting with all the links on the page:

```
a {
  text-decoration: none;   color: #544a40;
}

a:hover {
  text-decoration: underline;
}
```

First, we're placing our :hover styles after the existing global link styles. Although we didn't opt to use the :link, and :visited pseudo-classes, were we to use them, we would have to ensure that they were placed before our :hover styles. This is because all those pseudo-classes have equal specificity. We want the :hover styles to override the others, so they need to appear *after* any original :link and :visited styles targeting the same elements.

The other thing to notice is that we're changing the value of the text-decoration property. This is a common technique. So, as depicted in Figure 5.2, whenever a user hovers over any link on the page, the text in that link will appear with an underline.

Figure 5.2. The :hover pseudo-class in action

Causing an underline to appear on all text links on hover is fine for the footer links and the sidebar links, but the effect is not as visually pleasing on some of the other areas of the page, such as the main navigation and the text on the buttons. In order to target those and change them, we'll have to add some rule sets using :hover that are higher in specificity. Let's start with the main navigation:

```css
nav a {
  color: #fefefe;
}

nav a:hover {
  text-decoration: none;
  color: #cdb8a5;
}
```

In this new rule set, we're removing the underline on hover and changing the color to #cdb8a5 (which is a color sampled from the textured background of RecipeFinder). Because the header doesn't yet have a background color, the text will look as though it disappears on hover. This'll improve later in this chapter when we add the correct background.

Let's fix the :hover styles on the two buttons:

```css
.promo-btn:hover {
  text-decoration: none;
}
```

We're not adding any color change to the button text on hover. We'll do something different for them later on in the chapter. Lastly, let's correct the underline that appears below the linked text in all the entries in the "Latest Recipes" section:

```css
.media a {
  text-decoration: none;
}

.media a:hover h2,
.media a:hover p {
  color: #b32c1c;
}
```

These hover styles are a little different. In this case, we're targeting elements that are inside our <a> elements (the <h2> and <p> elements). So the :hover class is part of a selector that uses the descendant combinator (the space character). The text color chosen for the hover state is, again, a color sampled from the Photoshop file. In some cases, the original design may indicate hover states, but in this project we're using our own judgment to choose the hover states.

For now, that should cover some of the simple hover states we're adding to RecipeFinder. We'll add a few more later in this chapter when we tackle a few other techniques.

Transitions

A CSS feature that works nicely with the `:hover` pseudo-class is the transition property. The transition property allows you to change the values of CSS properties over a specified duration, animating the properties as they change from one state to another.

For example, look at the hover color changes we just added to the main navigation and the "Latest Recipes" section. Hover the mouse over those links and the color change happens instantly. With a CSS transition, we can make the color change occur gradually. Here's how we'll do it on the navigation links:

```
nav a {
  color: #fefefe;
  transition: color .4s ease-out;
}

nav a:hover {
  text-decoration: none;
  color: #cdb8a5;
}
```

This new declaration we've added is a shorthand property that represents the following longhand properties:

transition-property
This is where we identify the property we want to transition. In our example, we've defined the value as "`color`," meaning it will transition the color property. This value can also be "`all`," which means all properties that have a changed state (for example, via `:hover`) will transition.

transition-duration
This is the amount of time we want to occur while the property is changing from one value to another. It can be defined in seconds (as in our example) or milliseconds (e.g. 400ms).

transition-timing-function

This defines how the transition will proceed over the course of its duration, or, to put it another way, it defines the style, or manner, of the transition. This property can take a number of predefined keyword values, such as linear, ease-in, ease-out, and so on. It also accepts function values, which are a bit complex, so they are beyond the scope of this book. In most cases you won't need anything more than the simple, predefined functions.

transition-delay

This property defines how much of a delay should take place before the transition occurs—again defined in seconds or milliseconds. In our example, we did not include a value for transition-delay, so it just defaulted to a 0s delay, or no delay.

Looking back at the code we used to write our transition, now that we know all the longhand properties that make it up, we can alternatively write it like this:

```
nav a {
  color: #fefefe;
  transition-property: color;
  transition-duration: .4s;
  transition-timing-function: ease-out;
  transition-delay: 0s;
}
```

So, why are we putting the transition in the rule set that targets the links directly, rather than on the :hover state? Well, we want the transition to occur when the user moves their mouse over the links as well as when they move their mouse off. If we put the transition only on the :hover state, then the transition will occur only when the user hovers over the links, not when the user moves off. By putting the transition directly on the element itself, we ensure that the transition occurs in both directions: hover-on and hover-off.

Let's continue by adding a transition to the text links in the "Latest Recipes" section:

```
.media a h2,
.media a p {
    transition: color .3s linear;
}

.media a:hover h2, .media a:hover p {
    color: #b32c1c;
}
```

The first declaration block is the example we just added, with two grouped selectors. The second is included to demonstrate where the first example should be placed in our CSS file. With this new rule set added, the color change on the text links in the .media blocks should be gradual, rather than sudden.

Multiple Transitions on a Single Element

If we want to transition more than one property on a single element, we can't define multiple transition properties like this:

```
.example {
    transition: color .4s ease-out;
    transition: width .7s linear;
}
```

When a browser sees the same property defined more than once on a single element, the first instance of that property is ignored and only the second instance will have any effect.

So, to transition multiple properties on a single element, we have two choices. Firstly, we can use the all keyword, mentioned earlier. This will transition all properties. Secondly, we can define multiple transitions on a single declaration by separating them using commas, like this:

```
.example {
    transition: color .4s ease-out, width .7s linear;
}
```

In this example, both the color and width properties will be transitioned, and they will do so using different durations and timing functions.

Vendor Prefixes

If we include the code for transitions that we've just discussed, depending on the browser being using to test them, it's possible that the code won't work. Some browsers currently support CSS transitions using the standard syntax (which I just introduced), but other browsers require the use of an experimental prefix. To get this code working in all browsers that have support for transitions, we need to write it like this:

```
nav a {
   color: #fefefe;
   -webkit-transition: color .4s ease-out;
   -moz-transition: color .4s ease-out;
   -o-transition: color .4s ease-out;
   transition: color .4s ease-out;
}
```

Notice that, now, we are including four different lines of code for this single transition declaration. The -webkit- line is for Chrome and Safari browsers, the -moz- line is for Firefox, the -o- line is for Opera, and the last line (which has no vendor prefix, and which should always be included last), is for all browsers that support the standard syntax, including IE10.

Vendor prefixes are generally safe to use, but be aware that when new CSS features are still going through the standards process, there could be changes in the way the syntax works.

We don't have space in this book to describe all the quirks that could potentially occur when using vendor prefixes, so to learn more about which browsers support which features, and with what syntax, refer to Can I use...[1], which is an online searchable reference with support tables for all sorts of HTML, CSS, and JavaScript features.

It's also worth checking out a website called Prefixr,[2] created by Jeffrey Way, which lets you paste all your CSS into a text field and then generate all the necessary vendor prefixes to get the code working in as many browsers as possible. Remember

---

[1] http://caniuse.com/
[2] http://prefixr.com/

to back up original code before committing to anything that modifies it automatically like this.

So, for the remainder of this book, we will be using only the standard syntax for all the code. If something isn't working, check the Can I use... website to see if it's a browser support or vendor prefix issue that's the culprit. Failing that, try putting the code into Prefixr and then use whatever output it provides instead.

Transforms

In this next section, we're going to talk about a CSS feature that's quite complementary to transitions: CSS transforms. Transforms use the `transform` property along with a number of different transform functions to alter the look and/or position of elements on the page in various ways. A transform looks like this:

```
.example {
   transform: rotate(180deg);
}
```

The function used in that example is the `rotate()` function. Let's briefly cover functions available for use with transforms.

translate

The `translate()` function works much like the position property. Using it, or the related `translateX()` and `translateY()`, you can move an element along the x and y axes.

So if we had a box on the page that we wanted to move 20px to the left and 30px down from its original position, we could enter the following:

```
.box {
   transform: translate(-20px, 30px)
}
```

The first value in the `translate()` function defines the movement on the x axis (horizontal movement), and the second value defines the movement on the y axis (vertical movement). The alternative `translateX()` and `translateY()` functions define the x and y movement directly, each accepting a single value.

scale

The `scale()` function lets you change the size of an element by defining a pair of unitless numbers for the sizing along the *x* and *y* axes. Like `translate()`, the alternatives to `scale()` are `scaleX()` and `scaleY()`. So we could change the size of our box like this:

```
.box {
  transform: scale(1.2, 1.5);
}
```

This will scale the box up 1.2 times its size horizontally, and 1.5 times its original size vertically. If we were to scale the element by 1 or 1, 1, it'd have no effect because 1 represents the element's original size. If we leave out the second unit, it's assumed that the first unit defines both horizontal and vertical sizing. A value of less than 1 (such as 0.5) will scale the element down from its original size.

rotate

The `rotate()` function does exactly what the name implies—it rotates the element by a value defined in degrees:

```
.box {
  transform: rotate(45deg);
}
```

This will rotate the box 45 degrees clockwise. A negative value will rotate the box counter-clockwise.

skew

The `skew()` function, along with `skewX()` and `skewY()`, lets us distort the shape of an element along the x or y axes. So, for example, if we had a box that was sized at 200px by 100px, and we applied the following skew:

```
.box {
  transform: skew(-30deg, 10deg);
}
```

...then the result would look something like Figure 5.3.

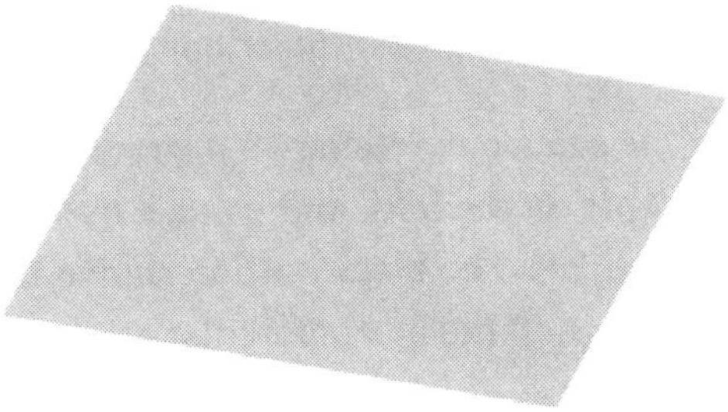

Figure 5.3. A box skewed with CSS transforms

Multiple Transforms on a Single Element

As is the case with transitions, if we want to apply more than one type of transform on a single element, we can't define multiple transform properties. Instead, we have to do the following, which is slightly different from how we accomplished this earlier with transitions:

```
.box {
    transform: scale(1.2, 1.5) skew(-30deg, 10deg);
}
```

This puts two transforms in a single transform declaration, separating the transform functions using a space (instead of a comma). With this syntax, the scale and skew transforms will both be applied to the targeted element.

Defining the Origin of a Transform

Whatever transform we're defining, we have the option to define a starting point for the transform. So, for example, if we rotate an element, by default the element will rotate exactly in the center. You can change the point of rotation using the `transform-origin` property:

```
.box {
    transform: rotate(45deg);
    transform-origin: 30px 20px;
}
```

Here we're rotating the box 45 degrees clockwise, but we're altering the point of origin for the rotation so it's 30px from the left of the box's boundaries and 20px from the top. So, the element will still rotate 45 degrees, but it will do so from a different origin point, changing the overall position.

Figure 5.4 demonstrates the same box rotated 45 degrees, but using the default transform origin (the example on the left), and using a transform origin of "30px 20px" (the example on the right). The black outline shown in each of the rotations represents the original position of the box before the rotate transform is applied.

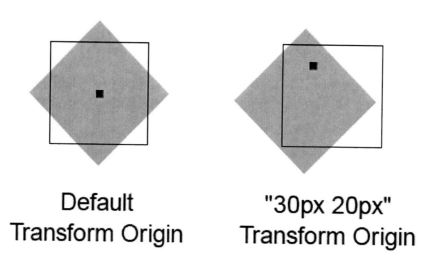

Default Transform Origin

"30px 20px" Transform Origin

Figure 5.4. The black outlines represent the original space occupied by the box; the small black squares represent the point of rotation

Combining Transitions and Transforms

All the transforms we've discussed so far are static. That is to say, their end result can be seen, but they won't animate to get there. The real power of transforms comes when combining them with transitions and animations. For RecipeFinder, let's incorporate a couple of transforms that will occur when the user hovers their mouse over certain elements.

First, we'll add to our styles to our two button elements:

```
.promo-btn {
  display: inline-block;
  width: 208px;
  padding: 13px 0;
  background-color: #6c0733;
  box-shadow: rgba(0, 0, 0, .25) 0 7px 2px 0;
  font-size: 20px;
  color: #fefefe;
  transition: transform .5s ease-out;
}

.promo-btn:hover {
  text-decoration: none;
  transform: scale(1.05);
}
```

Here we're applying a transition on the transform property, using a duration of .5s and a timing function of `ease-out`. When the user hovers over either of the two buttons, the specified scale transform occurs, increasing the size of the button slightly.

Now let's add a rotation transition to the Twitter icons in our "Yummy Tweets" section:

```
.tweet:before {
  content: url(../images/twitter-icon.png);
  display: block;
  position: absolute;
  left: 15px;
  top: 4px;
  transition: transform .5s linear;
}
.tweet:hover:before {
  transform: rotate(360deg);
}
```

This expands on our existing `.tweet` styles, adding a transition declaration to our `:before` pseudo-element, along with a new declaration block. The new declaration block uses something we haven't yet seen: two pseudo-selectors combined. In this case, we're telling the browser to rotate the :before pseudo-element element 360 degrees clockwise when the user hovers their mouse anywhere over a `.tweet` element (which contains the `:before` element).

Linear Gradients

The features described in this section will help us complete the overall look of RecipeFinder. CSS allows us to define graphics called **gradients**, without using images. A gradient is a static image that consists of two or more colors, where one is gradually changing into the other. Figure 5.5 shows what a basic gradient looks like.

Figure 5.5. A simple example of a gradient

Notice that the box in Figure 5.5 is not a solid color, but a combination of blue shades, with each gradually changing into the next.

With CSS gradients, we can fiddle with our gradients right inside the browser, altering them directly in our CSS, and avoiding the need to edit images in Photoshop or another image editor every time we have to make a change.

Let's first introduce linear gradients by adding the missing gradient to the header of RecipeFinder. Here's the code:

```
body > header {
  box-shadow: rgba(0, 0, 0, .25) 0 3px 2px 0;
  position: relative;
  z-index: 10;
  background-image: linear-gradient(#87053e, #560329);
}
```

Notice the new line we've added to this declaration block that we wrote in an earlier chapter. This is not a new CSS property, but is, instead, a linear gradient function included as a value on the `background-image` property. The first value inside the parentheses is the top color for the gradient. The second value is the final color for the gradient. The browser constructs the remaining colors on its own, gradually changing the color from the first color to the next.

For a linear gradient, you can include as many colors as you want, separated by commas. The browser will automatically distribute the colors (called color stops), evenly over the element's background, and then the in-between transitional colors will be constructed automatically, creating the "gradient" look. Figure 5.6 shows us what the header looks like after adding this new line of code.

Figure 5.6. Our header after adding a linear gradient

As we can see, by default, the gradient direction occurs vertically from top to bottom. For an idea of how different colors in a linear gradient are distributed, here's another example, using a rainbow of colors:

```
.box {
  width: 300px;
  height: 300px;
  background-image: linear-gradient(red, green, blue, yellow,
➥ purple, cyan, magenta, olive, brown);
}
```

Figure 5.7 shows what this would look like when rendered in the browser.

Figure 5.7. A ridiculous multicolored gradient that demonstrates color stops

That's a beauty, isn't it? Seriously, please don't ever do anything like that on your web pages! This should, however, demonstrate clearly how multiple color stops are rendered. But there's more to linear gradients than just defining colors.

Positions for Color Stops

As mentioned, when including colors in a linear gradient, the browser will distribute the colors evenly across the element, filling in the transitional colors automatically by default. With each color defined, however, we have the option to define a location for the color stop. With no color stop positions defined, the first and last colors listed will default to positions of 0% and 100%, respectively. Let's try defining some custom color stops:

```
  width: 300px;
  height: 300px;
  background-image: linear-gradient(red 10%, green 70%, blue 84%,
➡ yellow 90%);
}
```

Here, we've defined a percentage for each color. This tells the browser where on the element to place the color stop. This code would render in the browser as shown in Figure 5.8.

Figure 5.8. A linear gradient with custom-positioned color stops

Changing a Linear Gradient's Direction

In addition to color stops, we're also able to define the direction of the gradient, which, by default, is vertical, from top to bottom. To define a custom direction for the gradient, just include the direction prior to the set of defined color stops, before a comma. Here are some other linear gradient examples with alternate directions specified:

```
.box-1 {
  background-image: linear-gradient(to top, #87053e, #560329);
}

.box-2 {
  background-image: linear-gradient(to left, #87053e, #560329);
}

.box-3 {
  background-image: linear-gradient(to right, #87053e, #560329);
}

.box-4 {
  background-image: linear-gradient(33deg, #87053e, #560329);
}
```

If we leave out the direction (like we're doing on the RecipeFinder header), then the default is to bottom, which we can also define explicitly. The final example shown in the previous code block uses an angle unit of 33 degrees to define the direction. This can also be a negative value. A value of `180deg` would be equivalent to `to bottom` or leaving out the direction altogether.

Adding Multiple Gradients on a Single Element

Earlier in the book we dealt with adding backgrounds to elements using the `background-image` property. In this chapter, we've seen that gradients can be added as backgrounds using a special function that works as a value for the background-image property. But what if you want to have more than one background on a single element?

We can have multiple background images (and therefore multiple gradients) on a single element by comma-separating backgrounds using either the `background` shorthand property, or the `background-image` property. Here are two examples:

```css
.example {
  background: url(bg-1.png) no-repeat top left,
              url(bg-2.png) repeat-x top left;
}

.example {
  background-image: linear-gradient(black, white),
                    linear-gradient(blue, green);
}
```

If we use the longhand `background-image` property, we'll also have to comma-separate the values on the other longhand properties to match the backgrounds. This would get lengthy and hard to maintain using longhand, so it's always a good idea to try to use shorthand for background images, especially to incorporate multiple background images on a single element.

Adding More Linear Gradients

Now that we've covered the syntax for linear gradients, let's finish off the look of RecipeFinder. We have three more linear gradients that we need to add. First, we'll add the gradient for the promo button. The code will be the same as used for the header, because they use the same colors:

```
.promo-btn {
  display: inline-block;
  width: 208px;
  padding: 13px 0;
  background-color: #560329;
  background-image: linear-gradient(#87053e, #560329);
  box-shadow: rgba(0, 0, 0, .25) 0 7px 2px 0;
  font-size: 20px;
  color: #fefefe;
  transition: transform .5s ease-out;
}
```

For the promo button, the linear gradient declaration is placed immediately following the `background-color` declaration. We don't have to do this, but it often helps with code maintenance to group related CSS properties together. The background color serves as a fallback for browsers that don't support CSS gradients. It's important to remember to specify a background color to ensure your design remains readable in browsers that don't display the gradient. Figure 5.9 displays the promo button after adding the gradient.

Figure 5.9. Our promo button after adding a linear gradient

Next we have the gradient to add to the button at the bottom of the "Latest Recipes" section. Here's the code:

```
.more-btn {
  text-align: center;
  float: right;
  margin-right: 50px;
  width: 280px;
  background-color: #2d1e10;
  background-image: linear-gradient(#6b5139, #2d1e10);
}
```

Again we've added a fallback background color for non-supporting browsers and the linear gradient is just a simple top to bottom two-color gradient. Figure 5.10 shows us the button with the gradient.

Figure 5.10. Our second button with a linear gradient

The last gradient for the RecipeFinder website is going to be added to the small area that appears below the promo image. As discussed earlier in the book, we left that portion without a background so we could fill it in with a linear gradient in this chapter! Here's the code:

```
.promo {
  position: relative;
  z-index: 5;
  padding-bottom: 8px;
  box-shadow: rgba(0, 0, 0, .25) 0 3px 2px 0;
  background-image: linear-gradient(#4e0324, #4e0324 97%, #851f49);
}
```

Expanding on the styles for the .promo section, we've added a linear gradient to the background for that element. Recall that the .promo element is a wrapper for the section containing the big promo image. The eight pixels of bottom padding are what makes this section appear from behind the promo image.

The linear gradient consists of three color stops, with the second color stop being the same as the first. Also, the second color stop is positioned at 97%. This means the same color will appear on the background (behind the image, between 0% and 96%), up until the point where the padding starts, which is about 97% of the height of the .promo element. With this gradient in place, Figure 5.11 shows us what our promo section now looks like.

Figure 5.11. The small gradient below the big promo image

Radial Gradients

All the gradients on ReciperFinder are linear gradients, but CSS lets us create another kind of gradient—a **radial gradient**. A radial gradient creates a circular gradient. The syntax is similar to that of a linear gradient, but has some extra optional parameters. Let's look at a simple example:

```
.example {
  width: 300px;
  height: 300px;
  background-image: radial-gradient(pink, red);
}
```

That's as simple as it gets—a two-color radial gradient. The result in the browser would look something like Figure 5.12.

Figure 5.12. An example of a radial gradient

As with linear gradients, radial gradients let you specify positions for the color stops. By default, the first color listed will be at 0% and starts in the center of the element. Further color stops that don't have positions will distribute evenly moving outwards, with the final color stop positioned at 100%. So we could define multiple colors with custom color stops like this:

```
.box {
  width: 300px;
  height: 300px;
  background-image: radial-gradient(red 10%, green 70%, blue 84%,
➥ yellow 90%);
}
```

Again, this would create quite an ugly gradient, but it nicely demonstrates how to create gradients with color stops and custom positions.

More Options for Radial Gradients

Prior to the defined color stops in a radial gradient, we have the option to include a size, shape, position, and direction for the radial gradient. There are numerous options, so we won't cover them in detail here, but let's look at an example:

```
.example {
  width: 300px;
  height: 300px;
  background-image: radial-gradient(circle 200px at top left,
➡ red, pink);
}
```

A gradient with those specifications would look something like Figure 5.13.

Figure 5.13. A radial gradient with a custom shape, size, and position

Compare what you see in Figure 5.13 with the code in the previous code block. In the code, we defined the shape of the gradient as "`circle`" and sized it at 200px. We also specified that it should be placed in the top-left corner of the element. Figure 5.13 shows the circular area of the gradient with its center in the top left of the element.

As mentioned, we won't cover all the details for the radial gradient syntax here. Just recognize that for both linear and radial gradients, we have the ability to include some of these options prior to the defining of the color stops. Basically, the browser will look at everything that appears before the first comma and try to interpret it as a color. If it's not a valid color (hex, RGB, etc.), then it will try to interpret it as a direction (for linear gradients), or a direction, position, size, etc. (for radial gradients).

For a more detailed discussion of linear and radial gradient syntax, you can check out any of the following articles:

■ "CSS3 Radial Gradient Syntax Breakdown" on Impressive Webs[3]

■ "CSS3 Linear Gradient Syntax Breakdown" on Impressive Webs[4]

■ "Using Unprefixed CSS3 Gradients in Modern Browsers" on SitePoint[5]

■ "Unprefixed CSS3 Gradients in IE10" on the IEBlog[6]

 A Word on Gradient Syntax

The syntax for both linear and radial gradients has changed quite a bit over the years, and it's now quite complicated to get gradients working in all supporting browsers.

The resources linked at the end of the gradients section in this chapter describe both old and new versions of the gradient syntax. You can also find generators online that use older syntaxes. So if you're having trouble with the code for gradients, then know that you're not alone.

If you want to avoid all these headaches, you can stick to using only the new standard syntax, with no vendor prefixed lines, and provide image-based or single color fallbacks for non-supporting browsers.

Keyframe Animations

In the past, complex animations on web pages have been achieved using video, Adobe Flash, or JavaScript. In recent years, the CSS specification has added key-frame-based animations using pure CSS. A keyframe animation is the final touch we're going to add to RecipeFinder, and then the project will be complete.

What we're going to add to RecipeFinder is just a simple animation to make the RecipeFinder logo fly in from the left part of the screen and spin into place. Let's look at the code we're going to use, first of all on the .logo element:

---

[3] http://www.impressivewebs.com/css3-radial-gradient-syntax/

[4] http://www.impressivewebs.com/css3-linear-gradient-syntax/

[5] http://www.sitepoint.com/using-unprefixed-css3-gradients-in-modern-browsers/

[6] http://blogs.msdn.com/b/ie/archive/2012/06/25/unprefixed-css3-gradients-in-ie10.aspx

```
.logo {
  float: left;
  margin-left: 145px;
  margin-top: -34px;
  position: relative;
  top: 34px;
  transform: translateX(-800%);
  animation: logomove 2s ease-out 1s 1 normal forwards;
}
```

Here we've added two new lines to the `.logo` rule set. First, we're using a `translateX()` transform to move the logo element off the page. We use a negative percentage value to achieve this.

The next line is a new property—the animation property, which is a shorthand property. Let's look at what properties this shorthand represents:

animation-name

In our example, we've defined the animation name as `logomove`. This property accepts a custom name of our choosing. This name will be used again later in the animation keyframes code.

animation-duration

This is the amount of time we want the animation to take, from beginning to end, for each time that the animation runs. As with the duration on a transition, this takes a time value in seconds or milliseconds.

animation-timing-function

This is exactly the same as the timing functions for transitions, including `ease`, `ease-out`, `linear`, and so on. We're using `ease-out` in this animation.

animation-delay

The delay, which is another time value in seconds or milliseconds, tells the browser how long to wait before the first iteration of the animation. In order to have a delay, we must first define a duration. So, the second time value that's seen will always represent delay, whereas the first will always represent duration. This animation includes a small one-second delay to account for the time it might take for the page to finish loading.

animation-iteration-count   This is the number of times we want the animation to play. The default is 1, and we've defined it explicitly in our example, even though we didn't have to.

animation-direction   The animation-direction property defines whether we want the animation to play forwards or backwards. We've chosen `normal`—the default value, which means it will only play forwards. You can also define it with a value of `reverse` (to play it backwards), `alternate` (which alternates forwards then backwards each time the animation plays), and `alternate-reverse` (which starts playing it backwards on the first iteration, then alternates from there).

animation-fill-mode   The fill mode for the animation can be `forwards`, `backwards`, `both`, or `none` (the default). This tells the browser what styles to apply to the element after the animation completes. With a value of `none` or `backwards`, for example, our logo would fly in from the left, then, after it finishes, disappear to get back to where it started. We want it to finish with the styles that end the animation, so we define it as `forwards`.

Knowing all these details, we can choose to write our animation styles using longhand, like this:

```
.logo {
  animation-name: logomove;
  animation-duration: 2s;
  animation-timing-function: ease-out;
  animation-delay: 1s;
  animation-iteration-count: 1;
```

```
    animation-direction: normal;
    animation-fill-mode: forwards;
}
```

But as is the case with many CSS features, the shorthand is much easier to maintain because it uses less code, so we'll use that. While learning CSS it can be useful to use longhand for many properties, just to aid familiarity with each property individually. But eventually, it's almost always more practical to use the shorthand.

If we put that code into our CSS and refresh the page, we won't see anything happen. This is because we haven't yet defined any actual keyframes to accompany the animation property. Let's do that now.

```
@keyframes logomove {

  0% {
    transform: translateX(-800%) rotate(0);
  }


  100% {
    transform: translateX(0) rotate(-360deg);
  }

}
```

As shown here, keyframes are defined using the @keyframes at-rule. We learned about at-rules in Chapter 1. Notice, however, that this at-rule is a little different. Here are some points to help you understand this syntax:

- The @keyframes part is followed immediately by the custom animation name that we chose and included in the animation property.

- There is one set of curly braces that wraps the entire set of keyframes.

- Each keyframe block has a selector with another set of curly braces for each keyframe.

- Each keyframe selector is defined using a percentage.

A single keyframe represents how the element will look at that point in the animation. All the in-between keyframes that aren't defined are where the animations take place. So between keyframes the styles will transition, or animate, until they reach their state in later keyframes, using the duration we defined in the animation property to determine how long each phase of the animation takes.

The first and last keyframes are always 0% and 100% respectively, and they can be alternatively written as `from` and `to` respectively. If we don't include 0% and 100% (or `from` and `to`), then the browser will construct the first and last keyframes automatically.

Additionally, you can specify multiple percentages into a single keyframe selector, comma-separated, and even write the keyframes out of order. The browser will still render the animation in the order that is specified by the percentage keyframe selectors, regardless of the order in which they appear in the CSS.

With those keyframes in place, the logo will fly in from the left side of the screen and rotate as it appears, then settle in to its regular spot in the layout, as shown Figure 5.14.

Figure 5.14. The RecipeFinder logo animated using CSS keyframe animations

Graceful Degradation and Page Performance

A lot of the techniques we've discussed in this chapter are not supported in older browsers or, as is the case with gradients, are supported in older browsers using a different syntax.

If using any of these techniques, remember to test the pages without these features present, to ensure everything looks acceptable. This is a concept referred to as **graceful degradation**, meaning that the page will degrade gracefully, or without major problems, even if certain features don't work.

Another word of warning: many of these techniques, if used too liberally, can cause web pages to become slow and sluggish. For example, it may not be a good choice to layer multiple gradients on a web page's background. Similarly, too many animations can not only annoy users, but may also make your page slower than usual.

So use these techniques sparingly, and don't be afraid to resort to images if a CSS technique is causing the page to become too slow.

Other Cutting-edge Features

Since this is a short book, we can't possibly include every fancy new CSS technique, so we chose only the ones that have good browser support and that might be most practical.

Some other features that are worth looking into include:

- multiple columns
- values defined using `calc()`
- 3D transforms
- CSS filters
- CSS variables

You can get a basic overview and links to many new CSS features by checking out this page at Can I use...[7] or CSS3 Click Chart.[8]

---

[7] http://caniuse.com/#cats=CSS
[8] http://css3clickchart.com/

Making RecipeFinder Responsive

In Chapter 2, we touched on the concept of Responsive Web Design (RWD), and the use of media queries to achieve it. To close out this chapter, we're going to add some media queries to RecipeFinder to make it viewable on any size monitor, device, or screen. We're also going to change many of the pixel-based units in our existing CSS to use percentages instead.

With these new styles in place, the layout will adjust depending on whether the user is visiting the website on a desktop computer, a tablet (like the iPad), or a smartphone. In all cases, those visiting RecipeFinder will have access to the exact same information, but with an appropriate layout for each.

Before getting started, it's worth noting that we're going to run through all these changes and additions pretty quickly. This isn't a book on RWD, so we don't have the space to consider this topic in great detail. For a full discussion of RWD, check out *Jump Start Responsive Web Design*, also published by SitePoint.[9]

min- and max- Dimensions

There are four new CSS properties that we haven't discussed yet, and which often come in handy in flexible, responsive layouts. They are `min-width`, `min-height`, `max-width`, and `max-height`.

These work very similarly to the width and height properties except, instead of declaring the width or height explicitly, they set boundaries for them. For example, the first thing we're going to change in our styles is the width value declared for the `.center-global` elements:

```
.center-global {
  max-width: 1020px;
  margin: 0 auto;
}
```

Now, the width of `.center-global` will still be 1020 pixels, but when the browser window or device size is smaller, it will shrink to fit. Thus, it doesn't have a set width; it can be any width but it cannot be more than 1020 pixels.

---

[9] http://www.sitepoint.com/books/responsive1/

The other `min-` and `max-` properties work similarly. We'll use a few others in this section, and they'll often prove to be useful in responsive layouts.

Converting Pixels to Percentages

The next step is to convert all of our horizontal layout-based pixel values to percentages. By "horizontal", I'm referring to elements like left and right margins and padding, widths, and right and left positioning. The percentages we're going to replace them with will be percentage equivalents for the existing values. This means the layout will not change for standard, wide-screen desktop users.

Percentages in CSS are always relative to something. In the case of widths and left and right margins, these values are relative to the parent element's width. So if you have an element that is 100 pixels wide, and you add 10% of left padding to a child element, that 10% will compute to 10 pixels.

Let's begin with our `.logo` element, which is a child element of one of our `.center-global` elements (in this case, the one inside `<header>`):

```
.logo {
  float: left;
  margin-left: 14.2156862745098%;
  margin-top: -34px;
  position: relative;
  top: 34px;
  transform: translateX(-800%);
  animation: logomove 2s ease-out 1s 1 normal forwards;
}
```

Here we've changed the value for the margin-left property from 145px to a percentage value. This percentage is arrived at using the following formula:

target value / context * 100

In the case of the logo's left margin, the target value is 145 pixels. This was the amount of left margin we had on the element to begin with. We then divide that number by the parent element's width (the "context"). The parent element, as just mentioned, is 1020 pixels when it's at its widest. That calculation gives us a value of 0.142156862745098. The last thing we do is multiply this number by 100 (which

moves the decimal place over two places), giving us our final desired percentage—which in this case is about 14.22%.

 Too Many Decimal Places?

You'll notice the decimal-based percentage values we're using are specified using
an inordinate number of decimal places. There has been some discussion as to
whether this many decimal places is necessary. As it stands, it's probably only
necessary to include about three decimal places. But things could change in the
future, and browsers may require more decimal places to ensure higher-precision
results. Also, some people have noted slight changes in layout when removing
decimal places. It's likely, however, that the only real drawback to using this many
decimal places is the fact that it makes the CSS less readable at a glance. But we'll
put up with this for the purpose of ensuring that our layouts are as future-proof
as possible.

Let's continue changing pixel values to percentages. First, the right margin on the
<nav> element, which was 177px:

```
nav {
  float: right;
  margin-right: 17.35294117647059%;
  padding-top: 20px;
}
```

Next, the width and right values for the .promo-desc element:

```
.promo-desc {
  position: absolute;
  bottom: 93px;
  right: 7.35294117647059%;
  width: 30.98039215686275%;
  text-align: center;
}
```

The width value for the promo button (which is relative to the width of the .promo-
desc element):

```
.promo-btn {
  display: inline-block;
  width: 65.82278481012658%;
```

```
    padding: 13px 0;
    background-color: #6c0733;
    background-image: linear-gradient(#87053e, #560329);
    box-shadow: rgba(0, 0, 0, .25) 0 7px 2px 0;
    font-size: 20px;
    color: #fefefe;
    transition: transform .5s ease-out;
}
```

We won't change the width of the other button (.more-btn). We'll leave that at 280 pixels, which works fine since it doesn't have anything beside it.

Next, we'll change the width and padding values on the .latest element:

```
.latest {
  width: 62.74509803921569%;
  float: left;
  padding: 0 3.92156862745098% 0 3.92156862745098%;
  background: url(../images/bg-column.png) no-repeat top right;
}
```

... and so on. As long as we know the width of the parent element, then we can use the formula described earlier to get the correct percentage value. In some cases, we may have to account for inner horizontal padding when using percentages on nested child elements, but in most cases the calculation is pretty straightforward.

Using percentage values like this will help the layout adjust naturally when the elements are displayed on a smaller screen. For the remainder of our styles, go through and change all horizontal-based values (the widths, left padding, right padding, and any horizontal positioning using the left or right properties), from pixels to percentages, using the formula we discussed. After that, head on to the remainder of this chapter.

Fixing the Size of Images

Another thing we want to correct in our layout is the way the images look when the user is visiting the page with a smaller browser window or device. First, let's deal with the big promo image.

Let's add a line to our .promo styles:

```
.promo {
  position: relative;
  z-index: 5;
  padding-bottom: 8px;
  box-shadow: rgba(0, 0, 0, .25) 0 3px 2px 0;
  background-image: linear-gradient(#4e0324, #4e0324 97%, #851f49);
  overflow: hidden;
}
```

Here we've added the overflow property with a value of hidden. This is going to ensure that when the .promo element gets smaller, the big promo image that's inside it will not overflow the boundaries of .promo, but instead, any excess parts of the image will hide from view.

Then we'll add a new rule set that targets our promo image:

```
.promo img {
  width: auto;
  height: auto;
}
```

Here we're setting the width and height of the image to a value of auto to ensure the CSS overrides any dimensions set in the HTML using width and height attributes. If we didn't define a width and height in the HTML, then these styles wouldn't be necessary.

Next, we'll deal with the images inside the .media elements. Let's add three lines to the styles for those, in addition to the percentage value for the right margin:

```
.media img {
  float: left;
  margin-right: 4.6875%;
  max-width: 241px;
  width: 100%;
  height: auto;
  border: solid 9px #ede0d5;
  box-shadow: rgba(0, 0, 0, .25) 2px 2px 2px 0;
}
```

Notice we've added a max-width value of 241 pixels, combined with a width of 100%. This ensures that the image will fill 100% of its parent block container (the

`.media` element), but will not exceed 241 pixels. So when the browser width gets fairly small, the images will become smaller than 241 pixels, if necessary. We've also set the height to `auto`, as we did with the big promo image, which helps the height stay proportional to the width.

Adding Media Queries

In addition to percentages and max/min widths, to get a fully responsive website, we'll also need to add some media queries. We're going to use them to target four different browser widths. Each of these media queries target what are often referred to as "breakpoints":

```
@media (max-width: 930px) { }
@media (max-width: 730px) { }
@media (max-width: 480px) { }
@media (max-width: 340px) { }
```

Inside of the curly braces for each of these media queries, we're going to add whatever selectors and declaration blocks we need to make the layout adjust to the specified browser width.

Adding the Viewport Meta Tag

For every responsive design, you'll want to add the following HTML tag to the `<head>` section of your website:

```
<meta name="viewport" content="width=device-width,
➡ initial-scale=1.0">
```

Without this tag, the website will appear at normal width, but scaled down to fit the screen. This might not be desirable, so include this tag to ensure the media queries are working as expected. For a full explanation of the viewport meta tag, see the Mozilla developer site.[10]

As mentioned, since this is not a full discussion of RWD, we don't have the space to describe in detail all the layout changes we'll be making inside our media queries, but here is a rundown of what we'll do for each:

---

[10] https://developer.mozilla.org/en-US/docs/Mobile/Viewport_meta_tag

At 930 pixels ▓ Center the logo and drop the main navigation links below the logo.

▓ Disable the logo animation.

▓ Change the two-column layout in the main content area to a single column, dropping the sidebar below the "Latest Recipes" section.

▓ Change the width of each of the two columns to fill the available space (using width: auto) and remove the background on the left column.

▓ Change the 3-column footer to be a single column, again changing the three individual footer sections to width: auto.

▓ Change some margin, padding, positioning, and font values for various elements.

▓ Add a text shadow to the promo text so it's more readable when overlaying a light-colored promo image like the one we're using.

At 730 pixels ▓ Shrink the height of the promo image and realign the promo text and button.

▓ Add a border below each `.media` element to clearly delineate each entry in the "Latest Recipes" section.

At 480 pixels ▓ Change the padding on the main navigation items.

▓ Remove the float from the `.media` images so the accompanying text drops below each image.

At 340 pixels ▓ Make the main navigation links block elements (instead of inline-block), so they align vertically instead of horizontally.

The values chosen for these media queries (930, 730, 480, and 340) are not arbitrary, nor do they represent specific devices or commonly-used browser window sizes. These values are points at which the layout was breaking, and thus needed adjustments. These break points were discovered by resizing the browser window until the layout no longer looked readable or usable.

For each project, find out where the primary break points are, and then work from there, adding styles to the media queries after some trial and error.

To fiddle with these styles, view the CSS for the final version of RecipeFinder or download the code from the code archive for this book.

We can test RecipeFinder on a number of different devices to see if it works, or we can use an online tool that displays a URL in various widths, mimicking what happens in various devices sizes. One such tool is located at http://mattkersley.com/responsive/. Figure 5.15 shows us how RecipeFinder looks after adding our responsive styles.

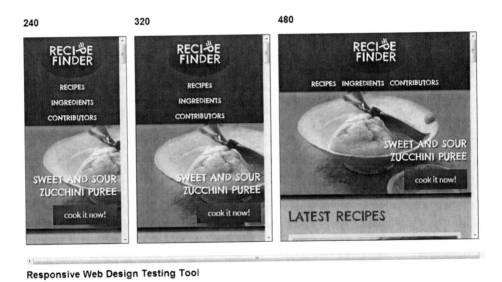

Responsive Web Design Testing Tool

Figure 5.15. RecipeFinder displayed using an online responsive design testing tool

Of course, a tool like this is only a guide and will not look and function the same as a mobile device. It's much preferable to test your projects on as many real devices as possible, but if budgets are small and the necessary hardware is hard to come by, these types of online tools are better than nothing.

Summary

At last, RecipeFinder is complete! We've looked at a number of cool techniques that can help add some life to our pages. With CSS gradients, animations, and transitions, we no longer have to resort to large unwieldy scripts and other troublesome techniques.

We've also scratched the surface of flexible layouts by making RecipeFinder responsive to different browser windows and device widths.

In the final chapter, you'll learn all about ways to debug and solve problems in code as quickly and as efficiently as possible.

Chapter **6**

Debugging Your CSS

The RecipeFinder project is complete and you now have a good, rounded understanding of what CSS is capable of, but there are some areas we haven't yet covered
that are well worth exploring.

In comparison to other programming languages, CSS is fairly simple, but it's not
without its quirks and inconsistencies. Firstly, as we've already touched on, not all
CSS features are supported in all browsers. Also, even where CSS code *is* supported
by all browsers, it's often implemented differently in one or several of them. This
is especially true when dealing with differences between older versions of Internet
Explorer and the other browsers (Chrome, Firefox, Safari, and Opera), or when using
very new CSS properties.

This chapter is not going to cover the specific browser compatibility problems that
are bound to arise at one time or another. Instead, we're going to look at how to
avoid and debug virtually all CSS problems, regardless of whether they are browser
issues, coding errors, or something else. These methods are universal, and should
help with many of the puzzling situations that you'll come across while writing
CSS.

Understand How CSS "Errors" Work

Write code that isn't valid, in many programming languages, and the result will be a syntax error warning, plus the program running the code will stumble at the error and won't run beyond that point. And so, until the error in the code is corrected, the program is effectively ruined.

CSS is different. For example, if we were to go to the top of the RecipeFinder stylesheet and add a bunch of random characters, then refresh the page in the browser, we'd notice only one change on the page: The `box-sizing` property that we added to the top of our stylesheet would no longer have any effect, causing, among other things, the sidebar to drop out of place.

Here's how the top of our stylesheet might look after adding some random characters that aren't valid CSS:

```
asdfjjlgkljd

* {
 -webkit-box-sizing: border-box;
 -moz-box-sizing: border-box;
 box-sizing: border-box;
}

.cf:before,
.cf:after {
    content: " "; /* 1 */
    display: table; /* 2 */
}
```

Here's what's happening. Instead of disabling the entire stylesheet, the random characters disable only the first rule set, which is the one using `box-sizing`. The reason only this first rule set is disabled is because the browser is viewing that first line with the random characters as a selector. So, what it does is read everything before the first curly brace, attempting to identify the elements you're trying to target. Since it can't identify those characters as a valid selector or selector group—or as anything else that's valid in CSS—it proceeds to ignore what's in that first declaration block.

Now look at this:

```
asdfjjlgkljd {}

* {
  -webkit-box-sizing: border-box;
  -moz-box-sizing: border-box;
  box-sizing: border-box;
}

.cf:before,
.cf:after {
    content: " "; /* 1 */
    display: table; /* 2 */
}
```

Here again we've inserted some random characters, but with one difference: we've added a pair of curly braces after the characters. In this example, the random characters will have no effect because the browser will ignore only what's inside the first set of curly braces (the empty ones). This is because the browser thinks the random characters are a CSS selector, so it reads the curly braces in that context.

Let's try something similar inside of a valid set of curly braces further down in our stylesheet. We'll remove the random characters at the top and this time we'll add a random group of characters inside the .center-global declaration block:

```
.center-global {
  asdfasdf
  max-width: 1020px;
  margin: 0 auto;
}
```

No prizes for guessing that this will cause only the max-width declaration to be disabled. As there's no semicolon at the end of the line of random characters, the browser views it as part of the second line, making it produce an internal error and ignoring the max-width declaration. But the rest of the CSS works just fine, because it appears after a valid semicolon at the end of the disabled line.

So what do we take from this? The basic principle to keep in mind is that *the browser will ignore any CSS it fails to understand but will continue to try to read the rest.*

Of course, there is a possibility, depending on which random characters are included, that they could disable the whole stylesheet. For example, a single opening curly brace at the top of the stylesheet would nullify the whole thing. The key is to understand that the browser is trying to read what's in between the curly braces (for declaration blocks), what's before each curly brace (for selectors) and what's before and after the colons and semicolons (for properties and values).

CSS Comments

Every programming language lets you add notes and other hints that help you understand what's going on. Not all CSS is as understandable at first glance as, say, something like `font-size: 20px`, so some sections of code can benefit from adding notes or other hints in their vicinity. We introduced the syntax for CSS comments in Chapter 2. You might remember this bit of code from our clearfix:

```
.cf {
  *zoom: 1; /* for IE6 and IE7 */
}
```

The comment in this line of code is the part that says "for IE6 and IE7," and is identifiable as such by the preceding backslash followed by an asterisk, and the asterisk and backslash at the end.

We can add as many of these to our stylesheet as we like, and it's good practice to use CSS comments to help identify parts of any stylesheet that might be difficult to understand from a cursory glance. By using CSS comments to make our stylesheets more readable, the CSS will be easier to maintain in the future.

A CSS comment can span multiple lines if required. Everything that's in between the opening and closing comment characters will be ignored by the browser, and so will the comment characters themselves. So often you'll see something like this in a CSS file:

```
/***************************
***************************
These are the styles for
the header section
***************************
***************************/
```

Notice that, in this example, not only have I included the opening and closing asterisk and backslash characters, but I've also added some extra asterisk characters spanning multiple lines. This makes the comment easy to find when scrolling through the CSS file. Add section headings like this in CSS to help organize it into readable, related chunks of code.

Unfortunately, CSS doesn't have an easy way to present a valid, single-line comment that uses just an opening comment character combo. For example, in JavaScript, you can comment out a single line of code like this:

```
// This is a JavaScript comment
```

This is helpful in JavaScript because it makes it easy to nullify an entire line of code, or add a helpful comment, with just two characters (the backslashes). But in CSS it's necessary to use both the opening and closing characters to specify the boundaries of any comments.

For quick, temporary fixes, however, it's acceptable to create a sort of *faux* CSS comment by applying the principle we discussed in the previous section on CSS errors. Let's say we have the following CSS:

```
.center-global {
  max-width: 1020px;
  margin: 0 auto;
}
```

And let's say we want to temporarily remove the first line (the max-width declaration). We could do this:

```
.center-global {
  /* max-width: 1020px; */
  margin: 0 auto;
}
```

This works fine, but a quicker way to achieve the same result is simply to put some random characters at the beginning of the line, like so:

```
.center-global {
AAAAmax-width: 1020px;
margin: 0 auto;
}
```

It's quick and effective, but don't ever leave your CSS like this on a live website. It's not valid CSS and should only be used in development for doing quick debugging.

Validating CSS

When encountering a problem in your CSS, it may help to ensure that your code is as valid as possible. The World Wide Web Consortium (W3C)[1] is a standards body that decides what is and isn't valid in CSS. W3C produce an online validation system that lists all the errors it finds in submitted CSS. This is a good way to ensure that any problem isn't due to a coding error. The CSS validator[2] enables users to validate their CSS using three options: by a URL (which is a link to the website in question), by uploading a CSS file, or by copying and pasting CSS into a text box. Use the latter option for any website you're working on that's only available on your local computer.

Now that we're done with RecipeFinder, we can use CSS Validator to see if there are any errors in our code. Figure 6.1 shows the result we achieve.

---

[1] http://www.w3.org/
[2] http://jigsaw.w3.org/css-validator/

W3C CSS Validator results for TextArea (CSS level 3)

Sorry! We found the following errors (7)

URI : TextArea

22	.cf	Parse Error *zoom: 1;
23	.cf	Parse Error }
112		Sorry, the at-rule @-webkit-keyframes is not implemented.
126		Sorry, the at-rule @-moz-keyframes is not implemented.
140		Sorry, the at-rule @-o-keyframes is not implemented.
180	nav ul li	Parse Error *display: inline;
185		Parse Error [: 30px; font-size: 20px; } nav ul li:last-child]

Figure 6.1. Running RecipeFinder through the validator

In addition to the seven errors that the validator finds, there are also 51 warnings. None of these errors or warnings has any visible effect on our page, no matter which browser we use, and with the exception of two examples, they're a result of using vendor prefixes like `-webkit-`, `-moz-`, and `-ms-`. This is fine. We don't need to worry about the validity of our CSS with these types of warnings.

For the most part, the validator is a guide. Don't expect to get perfect results. In fact, receive perfect results (no errors, no warnings), and the likelihood is that you're doing something out of the ordinary, such as not using any CSS features that have been introduced in the past few years. Also, remember to use the validator throughout the coding process, and not just at the end.

What about the other two CSS errors that aren't related to vendor prefixes? Those two errors are due to the fact that two of our CSS declarations begin with an asterisk character. Those asterisked declarations are CSS hacks. The first example is part of our clearfix code and the other helps us to align our navigation elements. Let's take a moment to consider these types of hacks.

CSS Hacks

As previously mentioned, this final chapter is not an extensive discussion of browser-specific issues, but it's important to be familiar with the concept of CSS hacks, as they've been valuable tools in many a CSS developer's box of tricks over the years.

A CSS hack is basically a line or block of code in a CSS file that only a specific browser, or browser version, understands. So if we run into a problem that only happens in one browser, we may have the option to use a CSS hack to target only that browser in order to fix the problem.

But a word of caution: A CSS hack should not be used unless all other possible valid solutions have been tried and exhausted. The rest of this chapter outlines some principles and techniques to help solve problems in CSS without the use of hacks. But as a last resort, for a list of possible CSS hacks, or to learn different ways to target older versions of Internet Explorer (which is the browser that's most frequently targeted by hacks), here are three articles to bookmark and refer to:

- "Conditional Stylesheets vs CSS Hacks? Answer: Neither!" by Paul Irish[3]

- "Browser [-specific] CSS Hacks" by Paul Irish[4]

- "How Do I Target IE7 or IE8 Using CSS Hacks?" by Louis Lazaris[5]

Reduced Test Cases

Reduced test cases are invaluable for debugging particularly knotty problems in CSS. A **reduced test case** is a bare-bones version that displays the same behaviour as the problem in question.

For example, perhaps there's an issue in one of several columns in a really complicated layout (where each column contains all sorts of content, such as images, text,

---

[3] http://paulirish.com/2008/conditional-stylesheets-vs-css-hacks-answer-neither/
[4] http://paulirish.com/2009/browser-specific-css-hacks/
[5] http://www.impressivewebs.com/ie7-ie8-css-hacks/

headings, and so on). To figure out what's wrong, we can try to reduce the content in that column and see if the problem persists.

Maybe we have a two-column layout and the problem area is in column two. We can try removing all the CSS or all the HTML inside column two, and leave only the CSS we're having the problem with, to see if that fixes it. If it doesn't, then we can try removing the HTML and/or CSS in column one, and see if that helps.

CSS comments will often come in handy in a case like that, so instead of deleting CSS, simply wrap the unwanted CSS in comments, removing it only temporarily, then adding those styles again once the issue has been chased down.

By systematically removing as much as possible while leaving only the problem HTML and/or CSS in place, it's easier to identify what causes the problem to go away. From here it's possible to narrow down even further by reducing single declaration blocks and, if necessary, by reducing single declarations.

Get Help Online

Even experienced developers cannot solve every problem immediately and without help. To resolve CSS issues, first remember that Google, as they say, is your best friend. Whatever problem you're having, it's almost certain that another user has had the same issue.

Type the problem into Google and see what results come back. Try entering the problem in the form of a question, or as a statement. For example: "How do I center multiple divs?" or "Right column falls below left column when using floats."

One website that'll almost certainly come up in many search results when looking for solutions to CSS problems is Stack Overflow.[6] Stack Overflow is a question-and-answer website frequented by thousands of experienced developers.

Another excellent source for finding answers to problems you're encountering in your CSS is the CSS section of the SitePoint forums.[7] There are thousands of archived forum posts to mine for information, and its membership includes a number of experienced CSS developers who are more than happy to help with problems.

---

[6] http://stackoverflow.com/
[7] http://www.sitepoint.com/forums/forumdisplay.php?53-CSS-amp-Page-Layout

Use Online Coding Tools

We've already talked about debugging problems by systematically reducing the issue to a bare minimum of code. In order to create real, live, editable, reduced test cases, there are a number of online tools well worth taking advantage of. A few of the most useful are JS Bin,[8] CodePen,[9] and jsFiddle.[10]

All of these sites make it possible to write code in one panel and view the result in another, on the same screen. This is great for creating reduced test cases, and then messing around with the code until the solution reveals itself. Conveniently, most of these tools update the code automatically as you type, too, so there's no need to keep hitting "refresh."

Ideal for experimenting with new or unfamiliar coding features, these tools are invaluable.

Test Your Layout Early in Multiple Browsers

Most developers do almost all their coding on a single project in one browser. Many choose Firefox or Chrome, both of which are good choices because of the extra tools they offer for development (see the next section). Be sure to check your layout in multiple browsers, soon after the basic framework is in place, and prior to adding lots of extra shadows, gradients, backgrounds, and so forth. It's much easier to fix problems early on, when you haven't yet committed to a lot of code. It might even be worth checking your CSS in multiple browsers at regular intervals. For example, check after finishing the header, then check again after completing one column in the main content area, and again after the next column, and so on.

If you know that many of your website visitors will be viewing the site in a particularly old browser (like Internet Explorer 7 or 8, or Firefox 3.5), then it's even more vital to check for layout differences early. Layout problems are much more difficult to correct in older browsers after having committed to a lot of HTML and CSS, so checking the results in those browsers very early in development, and often thereafter, will ensure you minimize problems.

---

[8] http://jsbin.com/
[9] http://codepen.io/
[10] http://jsfiddle.net/

Fortunately, layout issues are not as much of a problem with newer browsers like IE9 and IE10, and later versions of Firefox, Chrome, Safari, and Opera. But do check early to reduce the risk of having to rewrite a lot of CSS in later stages. Or, worse yet, having to rely on browser hacks to get the results you want.

For more info on principles and work flow that can help your CSS be as bug-free as possible, see the following two articles:

▨ "The Principles of Cross-browser CSS Coding"[11]

▨ "Cross-browser CSS Development Workflow"[12]

Use Developer Tools and a Good Text Editor

Here are two final tips that will help you reduce overall development time. The catch is that they require the use of some fairly complex tools.

The first tip is to know how to use developer tools in your browser of choice, and learn to use them to debug issues. If you use Google Chrome as a primary development browser, you'll have a set of developer tools that come pre-installed with the browser, seen in Figure 6.2. To open those tools, hit the F12 key, enter the alternate keyboard combination of CTRL-SHIFT-i, or right-click (Command-Click on a Mac) anywhere on a web page and select **Inspect element** from the context menu.

---

[11] http://coding.smashingmagazine.com/2010/06/07/the-principles-of-cross-browser-css-coding/

[12] http://www.impressivewebs.com/cross-browser-css-workflow/

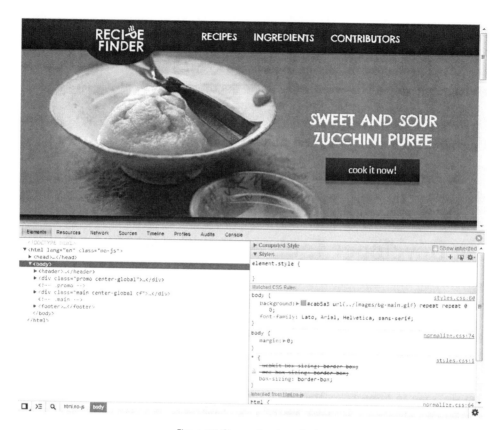

Figure 6.2. Chrome Developer Tools

Apple's Safari browser also comes installed with developer tools, as do Internet Explorer and Opera. For Firefox, you can download two add-ons to help with development: the Web Developer toolbar[13] and Firebug.[14]

The Web Developer toolbar appears in Firefox below the address bar, and includes a number of options, including many CSS-related features. The Firebug add-on, seen in Figure 6.3, works much like Chrome's developer tools, opening when you hit F12 or when you right-click (Command-Click on a Mac) an element on the page and choose **Inspect Element with Firebug**.

---

[13] https://addons.mozilla.org/firefox/addon/web-developer/
[14] http://getfirebug.com/

Figure 6.3. Firebug

Chrome's developer tools and Firefox's Firebug add-on conveniently display all the styles applied to the selected element, making it easy to change these on the fly right there in the browser, inside the CSS panel. The changes are applied to the page immediately and will remain until the page is refreshed.

This can be an excellent way to add small sections of code, and see the changes take place instantly, saving you the trouble of having to go back and forth between the text editor and browser, refreshing the page each time. And, as a bonus, after writing some code, you can then select the section you've edited and paste it into your real CSS file, knowing it will work as expected.

In Figure 6.4, you can see the live editing taking place, where an entire declaration has been removed (the background on the `<body>` element), and another has been edited (the `margin` value on the `<body>` element).

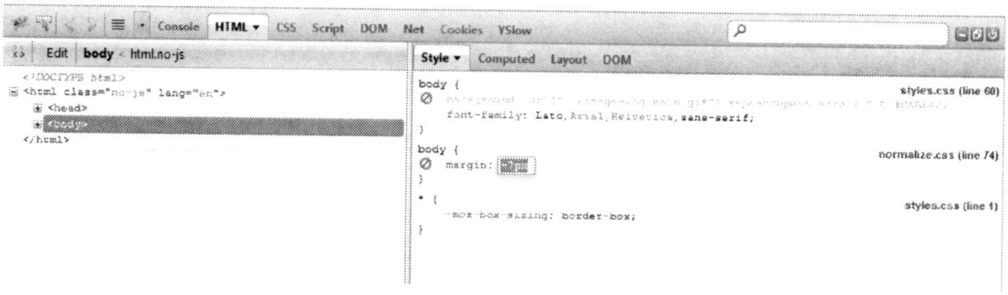

Figure 6.4. Editing in Firebug

In addition to learning how to use in-browser developer tools, the other tip is to find a good text editor and become familiar with its many shortcuts and features. This will boost your productivity and development speed. Some excellent and popular choices include Sublime Text[15] (PC or Mac, not free), Notepad++[16] (PC only, free), and Coda[17] (Mac only, not free).

There are others, too—some free, some not. In general, the text editors you have to pay for are quite good and well worth the relatively small, one-time cost.

Most importantly, these editors have tons of excellent coding features designed for front-end developers working primarily with HTML, CSS, and JavaScript. These include auto-complete functionality for typing CSS properties and values, options for different color schemes, enhanced search-and-replace functionality, and much more. So do yourself a huge favour by installing one of these editors, and slowly taking the time to learn about all its features.

In Figure 6.5, you'll see Sublime Text with a custom color scheme for syntax highlighting. You'll notice that Sublime Text recognizes the `float: left` declaration as typing begins, meaning all we have to do is hit the tab key and it will auto-complete the declaration. It also adds the trailing semicolon automatically!

---

[15] http://www.sublimetext.com/
[16] http://notepad-plus-plus.org/
[17] http://panic.com/coda/

```
.media img {
  float: l;
  margin-r left          */
  max-width: 241px;
  width: 100%;
  height: auto;
  border: solid 9px #ede0d5;
  -webkit-box-shadow: rgba(0, 0, 0, .2
  box-shadow: rgba(0, 0, 0, .25) 2px 2
}
```

Figure 6.5. Editing in Sublime Text

This book, however, is far too short to describe the true power of these kinds of applications. Try a good text editor out (even those that cost offer free trials), and fiddle with the features to really understand how good they are. Don't have the time for this? Try searching online for tutorials that describe the features of the text editor you're considering. The bottom line is that learning CSS isn't complete without a tool to do a lot of the heavy lifting for you. A good text editor will look after this, and will allow you to focus on getting the job done as quickly and efficiently as possible.

Summary

CSS debugging and problem solving is a way of life for many front-end developers. Although it can be a headache at times, view every debugging session as a learning experience that will make you a better developer in the future.

Learn to do many of the tricks mentioned in this chapter, and you'll notice your CSS skills will improve dramatically with every project. Debugging CSS can actually be fun, especially when you understand why problems occur and start to apply the most productive and future-proof techniques to solve them.

CPSIA information can be obtained at www.ICGtesting.com
Printed in the USA
BVOW06s0405241013

334538BV00002B/2/P